HATS
Reflections on Life as a Wife, Mother, Homeschool Teacher, Missionary, and More

Elizabeth M. Trotter

Table of Contents

Foreword

No matter your background or experiences, being a woman is hard.
That's partly because being a human is hard. It's also due to the many
roles we women tend to carry in life. Daughter, sister, friend.
Professional, mother, wife. Marriage and motherhood are indeed holy
vocations, and they require much of a woman. Whether we work
outside the home or from within it, our vocations sometimes stretch
us so much that we fear we will break.

The truth is, there's not a lot of preparation for marriage or
motherhood. Certainly, we can read books. We can read books on
how to have a great sex life or how to build a godly marriage or how
to live out biblical submission, but when it really comes down to it,
we marry a human person, not a book, and our husbands also marry
a human person – us. A lot of marriage is simply trying new ways of
doings things and seeing if they work (including, at times, seeking
professional or pastoral help).

It's the same with motherhood. We can read books on natural
childbirth, healthy homemade baby food, and the most godly
parenting – or the most logical. But nothing can really prepare us for
meeting our child, some mysterious arrangement of our own DNA,
or someone else's. No one can prepare us for their likes or their
dislikes, their strengths or their weaknesses. We have to discover
these things for ourselves, over time.

What follows in this book is precisely that: the things I've discovered
over time. There are articles and essays on marriage, motherhood,
homeschooling, and the Christian life. In case you don't know me,
here's a bit of background: As of this writing I've been married for
nearly 18 years, having gotten married at the age of 18. I've been a

ministry wife almost that entire time and have been living overseas as a missionary wife for the past 6 years. I've been a mom for 14 years and have been homeschooling for 9. This book is my lived experience wearing all those hats.

Elizabeth M. Trotter

Phnom Penh, Cambodia
May, 2018

The Mom Hat

THE CHURCH: "I'M NOT THE ONLY ONE"

I always feel so discouraged about motherhood on Sundays. Sundays completely wear me out, taking care of my youngest children's needs. I feel so out of my league. I think about all the mom blogs out there and wonder how these women have all this energy just to spend on their kids' intellectual and spiritual development? I've got sin issues of my own that need working out; how can I give 110% to each kid???

Once I confessed this to another mom, who surprised me by confessing the same thing back. I felt so relieved. (And so did she.) I told her that every Sunday I think I'm not cut out to be a mom, and she told me, "Every day I think I'm not cut out to be a mom." So we lamented together, and we laughed together, and I was so relieved to know **I'm not the only one who thinks she's failing in this motherhood venture.**

One Sunday I was feeling particularly discouraged about motherhood. My husband was praying with and ministering to teenagers. This is something I love doing *with* him, and I miss it. (For our family's sake, I stepped back from youth ministry when I became pregnant with our third child.) So instead of participating in shiny, glittery youth ministry, I was responsible for the mundane task of picking up my kids from their Bible classes — and proceeding to keep an eye on them afterwards. That morning in particular, **I had an intense feeling of missing out on the good stuff.**

I sat there, all alone and lonely, when another woman came up to me and started a conversation. Suddenly I didn't feel so lonely. As we talked and shared about life, I discovered that she, like me, needed some encouragement. That she, like me, dislikes conflict. I felt so relieved. I'm not the only one!? I had been feeling so useless. And I thanked God for His kindness: He sent me one of His own to encourage me. He didn't have to, but He did. And neither did He let me walk out of church that morning feeling as utterly useless as I had begun.

One day I was surprised to hear a Christian I really respect talk about the struggle to find time for God in the chaos of overcommitment. I

2

literally breathed a sigh of relief. I'm not the only one!! When I accept too many social or ministry commitments, I struggle to find time to spend with God. And it's hard for me to say ?\"no" I felt less like a failure knowing that someone I love and respect also struggles with setting boundaries with their time. I felt less like a failure knowing I'm not the only one whose overcommitments interrupt their tight connection with God.

I tend to look at Christians I respect and think they don't have struggles anymore. I tend to white wash their humanity, to view them through a lens so hazy I can't see any flaws, to assume that one day, they just "arrived" and must surely be consistent in fighting against sin and in consecrating their time to God. **But I'm always relieved when I learn I'm not alone in whatever struggles I happen to be facing.**

Community with other believers is where we learn we're not alone. Ah the joy and relief of these moments. Nothing compares. These moments are the ties that bind. They are the mutual woes, the mutual burdens we bear. We share our fears, our hopes, our aims, our comforts, and our cares.* **It's what I love about the Church.**

From John Fawcett's hymn "Blest Be the Tie That Bind"

~~~~~~~~~~~~~~~~~~~~~~~~~~~~~~

"Not far away from us, there is someone who is afraid and needs our courage; someone who is lonely and needs our presence. There is someone hurt needing our healing; unloved, needing our touching; old, needing to feel that we care; weak, needing the support of our shared weakness.

One of the most healing words I ever spoke as a confessor was to an old priest with a drinking problem. 'Just a few years ago,' I said, 'I was a hopeless alcoholic in the gutter in Fort Lauderdale.' 'You?' he cried. 'O thank God!' When we bring a smile to the face of someone in pain, we have brought Christ to him."
Brennan Manning

THE THING THAT HAPPENED WHEN I WAS SCRUBBING THE KITCHEN FLOOR

It was many years ago now. My boys were preschoolers, and my girls weren't even conceived. I was literally on my hands and knees scrubbing my kitchen floor with an old toothbrush when I got the call: the call from a university professor offering me an interview for a chemistry lab instructor position.

For a bit of background here, let me just say that I've loved chemistry ever since I walked into Mr. Smith's 10th grade chemistry class over twenty years ago. I love the ingenious organization of the periodic table, I love the way chemical reactions balance *just so*, and I love learning about how the smallest structures in creation affect large-scale life.

I always want more chemistry in my life, but with two young boys to take care of, such chemical thoughts were few and far between. So I cannot explain to you just how much I wanted this job. I would run the lab, prepare the chemicals and equipment, instruct the students, and grade their lab reports. It was an ideal part-time job for someone like me — someone with a love for chemistry but lacking both substantial experience and a graduate degree in my field.

Now, I had worked (very) part-time at the college chemistry level before, tutoring chemistry about five hours per week at a community college. And even that I had given up so I could stay home and nurse my newborn second son without interruption. Then suddenly I was handed this new opportunity — and from a prestigious private university no less.

The hours required for the job were somewhere between 10 to 20 hours per week. I had gone in for the interview hoping it would be fewer hours than that, but it wasn't. Both financially and family-wise, it was too many hours for me to take on. I simply couldn't afford that time outside the home, and I knew God was saying NO to this particular opportunity.

The interview had occurred, painfully enough, when my husband was out-of-town on a work/ministry trip. I was alone with two little boys when I heartbrokenly realized I wouldn't be able to take this job. I was alone with no one to comfort me in my obedience. I was alone as I cried so hard I couldn't breathe. I was alone when it seemed to me that my world was ending. (I thought it might be my last chance to grab a chemistry job before too many years elapsed and I was "unemployable.")

But I knew God's message to me was clear. For my family, and in that time, I needed to focus my full-time energies at home. And the funny thing about that experience? I never once longed for outside work again. I was really content at home and went on to have more babies (those aforementioned darling little girls). Obeying in the moment was *hard*, but the fruit in my daily life was lasting.

So what does obedience mean for me today? Because in the eleven years that have ensued since my kitchen floor story, my passions haven't waned a bit. I still want to do ALL THE THINGS. And I want to do all the things NOW.

I want to doula, and I want to write, and I want to edit, and I want to teach calculus, and I want to teach chemistry, and I want to do youth ministry, and I want to do women's ministry, and I want to spend more time reading to my kids, and I want to spend more time with my husband, and I want to spend more time taking care of myself.

But I can't do all those things at once. I can't even do many of those things at once. And I'm currently coming out of a season of discerning *which* things I need to be doing and which things I need to be saying "no" to. It's been a hard season. Not break-my-heart-hard like it was several years ago, just plain hard.

For me today, obedience means looking at the people who are *already* in my life, and saying yes to THEM. It means saying no to certain other things. I'm finding that as I practice my *yeses* and *nos*, I'm more content in each moment. I'm more joyful in each moment. I'm more present in each moment.

5

But make no mistake: saying both the *nos* and the *yeses* has been hard. Contenting myself in my current stage of life has been a slippery path to plod. Obedience isn't as clear this time, and there's not just one monumental decision to make. In its place are a multitude of tricky choices and subtle attitude adjustments. I hope practice makes these choices, if not perfect, at least a little easier.

Because in my mind's eye, I can still see myself on my hands and knees scrubbing the dirt out of an old linoleum floor with a toothbrush, listening to the ring of a landline telephone, and continuing to scrub as I answered it. I can still see the hope in my young heart when given the opportunity to do something I loved. And I can still see that nervous young mom walk into the chemistry building — then under construction — and wait, and pray.

I can still see me walking out of the building when the interview concluded and knowing, *knowing* that I couldn't say yes. I can still see me crawling into my boiling hot, broken-down 1988 Honda Civic and trying to catch my breath from the disappointment.

I can still see me calling my out-of-town husband, unable to stop the flow of tears, and hearing him tell me with love, "I'm so proud of you."

But best of all, I can still see myself enjoying full-time young motherhood in a crackly, crinkly 60-year old parsonage, day in and day out, for the next five years.

Those images are, for me, a symbol of choosing the best thing now, of choosing life for my family, of obeying even when it's hard. I hope and pray I take those images of wisdom and love with me through the rest of my mothering years, because that kind of joy is something I don't want to miss out on.

THESE ARE THE (MON)DAYS OF OUR LIVES

[From our second year in Cambodia.]

My daughter is a slow hand-washer. She does not want help and likes to do it all by her lonesome three-year old self. She, like Peter, not only washes her hands, but her face, and legs, and back, and tummy, and feet, and hair, as well. Her thoroughness consumes about 20 minutes a pop. She leaves the bathroom dripping wet, and has a tendency to slip or cause others to slip with her excess water. We are trying to teach her not to do this.

This morning she was washing her hands at the sink, and it started leaking a large amount. (It always leaks a small amount, this being, as you know, Cambodia.) Turns out her body weight had disconnected the sink from the drain below it. The sink was now wobbling.

Upon further inspection from Papa the Plumber, we discovered that not only had the pipe not been installed correctly in the first place (a common occurrence here), but also that *someone's* children had been sticking straws down that very sink. The straws being subsequently removed, Plumber Man was able to reconnect all parts, and even, impressively, screw them together correctly.
Leak solved.

****

Later the kids were watching a Khmer language video, and I heard a blood curdling shriek. Not the sound of kids arguing, which often happens during Khmer lessons, much to the disappointment of this wannabe mommy blogger who uses that one hour of precious time to try and hammer out some coherent thoughts. Oh no, this was a MUCH scarier sound.

The boys were screaming, "Her finger! String! Her finger's stuck on some string!!" I ran in, and looked, and sure enough, my other daughter had wrapped a string around her finger. The top third of her index finger was already dark purple, and the threads looked deep. I told the boys to go get the scissors, but I was able to untangle

7

it before they returned.

When I could breathe again, I took her to Plumber Man/School Nurse to examine the injury. He assured me that her finger would recover, and that in this case, he would not need to reconnect all parts.

SOMETIMES WE EAT CEREAL FOR DINNER

Some days I spend hours reading aloud with my kids. Sometimes that means science doesn't get done. Other days we pore over science books for hours, but grammar doesn't get done. Some days we get all the subjects done, but I run out of time to prepare dinner. On days like those we eat cereal for supper. But only if we have milk in the house.

Or we might eat peanut butter and jelly sandwiches for supper. But only if we have bread in the house. Because even with dedicated weekly meal planning and shopping trips, I can rarely keep enough bread or milk in the house. Which makes for a lot of husband-texts like "please pick up bread or we won't have supper" and "please get milk or there will be no breakfast." If all else fails, I pop popcorn.

Some days not every school subject gets done, but I dance with my younger kids and laugh at my older kids' jokes. Other days I put in a good, solid school day with the kids and feel satisfied but much too tired to write. I'm almost always too tired to exercise. Mostly I force myself to work out. I know from experience what happens if I don't. Sometimes I don't get to my email for weeks. Or I go for weeks without having time or mental energy to write. In those times I can really become unpleasant to live with.

Sometimes I go months without spending time with my closest friends. Sometimes I have so many social, school, and ministry engagements that I don't get sufficient time by myself to be a kind, sane person. Sometimes I'm so worn out by all this busy rushing that I lock myself away and skimp on spending time with my husband. Other times I choose to hang out with my husband regardless of what else "should" be getting done. And nothing does get done, but I sure am happy. I have discovered, in fact, that husband time is the biggest key to my happiness.

Sometimes I bemoan the fact that I can't do everything all the time. That I can't seem to get my life in order and pull myself together and *balance all the needs.* But maybe I'm not supposed to. Maybe every day isn't supposed to contain every thing. Maybe each day is only supposed to contain some of the things. Maybe something is always going to fall through the cracks.

And maybe I'm supposed to be ok with that.

WHAT I WANT TO GIVE MY TCKS

I didn't know how hard it would be to parent Third Culture Kids. I assumed that my own TCK upbringing would make it easier; I was only partially correct. While it's true that we share common feelings and experiences, and that my kids enjoy hearing stories from my own TCKhood, I didn't foresee the way living overseas would duplicate the pain of my youth. The grief of constant goodbyes, the temporariness of our community, the missing of friends and family back "home" – all these things deplete me.

I didn't know I'd need to juggle my own complicated emotions at the same time as my children's. It's hard for me not to outlaw my own emotions or to give my kids the time and space they need to grieve and mourn their own losses. I want to find the silver lining too soon, to rush too fast to a happy ending. It's hard not to swoop in prematurely in an attempt to ease their pain.

So in times of emotional distress, I actually tell myself to shut up. Then I open my arms and give them space to cry. I open my ears and give them time to speak. I want to give them a safe place to express themselves and to process their own emotions. I don't do this perfectly by any means, but it is my heart's desire nonetheless.

There's something else I want to give my TCKs, and that's *privacy*. I've chosen a very public profession; my children, however, have not. They may go wherever I go and live wherever I live, but they didn't choose to live a public life the way I did. Perhaps when they're grown, they will. I don't know. I only know I want to give them the luxury of choosing it for themselves.

Not too long after moving to Cambodia, I decided to keep my children's lives and struggles offline. I pulled back from sharing things about them on social media, and I focused on telling my own stories, and not theirs, on my blog. I'm guided by my own mother's example in this. Some of you know I struggled with an **eating disorder** as a teenager. I'm open about it now, but I would have been mortified if my mom had shared it publicly *then*, and I'm thankful for the way she protected my privacy.

I'm absolutely in love with my TCKs. They're amazing — so amazing, in fact, that they deserve to grow up out of the public eye. They're public enough as it is. That doesn't mean I'll never tell a story about homeschooling or family life, or share photos from a vacation or outing. But it does mean that, especially as they grow older and barrel towards middle school and high school, I try not to post private details about their lives. It means I think carefully before sharing about them, and that in any public discourse, you'll find me honoring them by accentuating the positive rather than the negative.

None of this means I don't have trusted real-life people to whom I turn for prayer and parenting advice, because I do. And it doesn't mean we don't have a sending organization and a sending church that are checking up on us and making sure that our whole family is thriving, because we're blessed to have both. And it most certainly doesn't mean we don't celebrate our children and their hilarious antics with our family and friends. Because we do! That's one of my favorite parts of family life, in fact, and we have a private Facebook messaging group for our closest family and friends just so we can share their sweet words and funny stories across the continents.

I love these words from fellow blogger and overseas worker Lindsey Lautsbaugh: "If people want to share their good news on Facebook and bad news in person, what's it to you? That actually sounds pretty healthy to me. 'Keeping it real' does not need to be an occasional #hashtag. If I see only people's success and not their struggle, failure, and fights with their kids, then I assume someone else gets the privilege of seeing those glorious moments. Someone else gets to gently say, 'Let your children live to see another day, walls can be re-painted.' Someone else gets to say, 'Call the counselor, and I'll babysit for you and your husband tonight.' Another friend gets to challenge our tendency to hide our weaknesses and struggles."

In saying all this, I recognize that different families do things differently. Some families may be more comfortable sharing their kids' stories publicly – and I don't judge that. All I want to do today is share my own personal parenting philosophy: I respect your right to feel your feelings, and I respect your right to keep those feelings private. *Those* are the things I want to give my TCKs.

I remember reading *The Witch of Blackbird Pond* by Elizabeth George Speare to my kids and feeling such a kinship with the main character Kit. She'd lived a life of privilege with her wealthy English grandfather on the island of Barbados, but when he died, she discovered his large debts. In order to pay the debts, she sold all his belongings.

After that she didn't know what else to do, so she booked a passage to New England, where some of her Puritan relatives lived. Her cousins' conservative lifestyle and religious customs were completely alien to her. When the ship docked on the shores of Connecticut, Kit realized **"There was something strange about this country of America, something that they all seemed to share and understand and she did not"**— a TCK moment if ever I saw one.

Kit suffers intense culture shock. She's already grieving the loss of her grandfather, and she now doesn't fit into Puritan culture. In some ways she's even rejected by the community. She doesn't understand their religion or their worldview, and friends are hard to find. Her uncle is particularly cold towards her, and she's never performed such difficult, backbreaking labor before. New England winters are brutally cold and long. She misses leisurely tropical island life in Barbados: the heat, the sunshine, swimming in the ocean, her grandfather's extensive secular library.

But she grows to love her extended family. She even grows to love the beautiful fields nearby. Towards the end of the book, Kit attends a wedding. She thinks about how she doesn't fit in in New England, even though she loves the people and the place: **"An almost intolerable loneliness wrapped Kit away from the joyous crowd. She was filled with a restlessness she could not understand. What was it that plagued her with this longing to turn back?"**

She had previously decided to return to Barbados and search for work there, but as she continues reflecting on both her old life and her new life, she realizes she can't go back to the way life was with

14

her wealthy grandfather. Her two cousins have both fallen in love, and she realizes that she has as well — only the man she loved wasn't a Puritan permanently rooted to the Connecticut soil. **He was a sailor, a migratory man, a man of good character, a free spirit like herself.** And he loved her back. "Home" for her would be anywhere he was. Marrying him would mean continually traveling between Barbados and Connecticut, always on the move, but always with him. **Literally, and not just figuratively, she was going to live in the In Between.**

Our home school curriculum chose this novel for its relation to the Salem Witch Trials in early American history, **but for me it turned out to be a metaphor for the life of the TCK.** Crossing cultures, never completely identifying with one culture, never fully belonging, always grieving a loss of some sort, but needing, so desperately needing, someone to love, care for, and understand her. So with that story in mind, I offer this prayer:

My child, I'm well aware that in this life, not everyone gets married.
But should you happen to marry, first and foremost I pray you will marry a fellow lover of Jesus.
And then — oh then I pray you will marry someone who feels at home in the In Between spaces, who knows how to live in the margins of life, who's comfortable crossing over and blending in,
even if never quite fully.
I pray you will marry someone with a wide view of the world, who doesn't think you're crazy
for your wide view, either.
I pray you will marry someone who looks to God for full identity and belonging, someone who will understand your need to do so as well.
I pray you will marry someone who understands the pain of separation and of goodbyes,
someone who shares your yearning for heaven.
I pray you will marry someone who understands that love is the best kind of medicine
for a hurting heart and who knows how to give it.
That person doesn't have to be a TCK, though they might be. Your Papa isn't a TCK,

15

but he understands loss and living in the fringe. He understands love and nuance.
So I pray for you to experience what I have experienced myself: that your heart
will be
fully understood and accepted, fully loved and wanted, fully celebrated and cared
for.
I pray you will have many years of adventure together, tasting of a perfect heaven
here on a very imperfect earth, each year growing ever closer to our God and to
each other.

The Wife Hat

WHEN MINISTRY AND MARRIAGE COLLIDE

Jonathan and I have been married almost 18 years now, and I can honestly say being married to him is the best thing that has ever happened to me. We were friends first, then fell madly in love our senior year of high school. Even our first year of marriage – considered by some to be quite difficult – was pure bliss. And I can honestly say that every year after that has grown more joyful and more intimate. This is not to say, however, that we haven't ever struggled.

I've shared before about two of the major struggles in my marriage. I've talked about how I didn't want to move overseas in the first place and how Jonathan and I were at an impasse until God got a hold of me. I've also shared my struggle to believe God loves me as much as my husband, since he seemed to have so many more gifts than I have.

There is another difficult season in my marriage that I've never discussed before. The two stories I mentioned earlier represent enormous works God wanted to do in my heart and in my spirit. They also had enormous implications in the way I lived everyday life alongside my husband. The struggle I'm going to talk about today might seem more earthy than spiritual, but it still looms quite large in the landscape of my memory.

Some of you know we served in youth ministry in the States for 10 years. At one point we lived in a Parsonage next door to the church building, and we hosted summer youth meetings in our house. Initially we only invited juniors and seniors to our house on Tuesday nights for Bible study, and I thoroughly enjoyed it. Later we started hosting all ages in our house every Wednesday night during the summer. And every Wednesday night without fail, teenagers trashed my house.

This went on for two whole summers. My house was a disaster every Wednesday night, and I had a breakdown every Wednesday night. Jonathan and I could not see eye to eye on this issue and often fought over it. He felt we needed to have the teens in our home, and that I needed to *want* to have them in our home, and that furthermore, he believed the teens would perceive my reluctance to welcome them into our home, so I needed to check my attitude.

This, as you can imagine, led to lots of stress in our marriage. I wasn't confident enough to instruct the teens how to throw trash in the trash cans or how to avoid spilling coke all over my white living room carpet. I'm more confident now and would be able to teach teenagers in that way, but I was too intimidated back then. (Also I was much more uptight about cleanliness when I only had two kids as opposed to now, with four.) I just wanted my husband to kick the teenagers out; I wanted him to do it for me. At the same time I felt an intense pressure to let them in my house every Wednesday, or else I'd be a "bad ministry wife."

Conflict can happen, even when you're married to your best friend, even when you are absolutely convinced he's the only one for you, even when you love practically everything about him. We shouldn't be surprised when we have disagreements with our spouses. We're different people, and we'll see the world differently. And when we feel our own point of view so strongly, it can be difficult to imagine someone else's point of view.

For any of my old darling youth group members who may be reading here today, please know **I love you**. And I want you to know I miss you all so dreadfully. I'm recounting a problem that was *mine*, not yours. Probably any of you who still like me enough to read my blog wouldn't have been the ones tearing it apart in the first place, but either way, it doesn't matter. This conflict wasn't about you.

Two years and many, many fights later, we finally got creative in our problem-solving. We finally thought outside the box. **This wasn't either/or.** It wasn't: have them at our house, or they won't feel the love. It wasn't: have them at our house, or I'm a failure. It was: let's have them *at* our house and not *in*. We didn't cancel Wednesday nights at the Parsonage. Instead, we invited teens into our yard (but outside our house).

We gathered around the fire pit for hot dogs and marshmallows, for long chats and pyromaniac adventures. We played volleyball with the teenagers and let all the youth volunteers' kids play in our kiddie pool. We swung on the bag swing and climbed up the rope on the oak tree. **And it was a great compromise.** It was hotter outside than in, that's for sure, but my husband didn't have to give up teens at his house, and I didn't have to give up my sanity, my privacy, or my clean house.

I share this story to illustrate that compromises around ministry stressors are possible. For a long time, I saw the problem one way, and Jonathan saw it another way, and as long as we did that, there was no meeting in the middle. We had to get desperate enough to think about things in a different way, desperate enough try something new. I'm such a black and white thinker that our eventual solution never occurred to me (or my husband). In the end he must have figured he had to do *something* about his unhappy wife, no matter the ministry cost.

Now I look back and think how silly we were that we couldn't find a compromise sooner. At the time, though, it didn't feel silly at all. It felt deadly serious, as I'm sure all marriage conflicts do at the time. It took me a long time, but it was a good lesson to learn: sometimes there's a solution that isn't either/or. Sometimes there's a solution that meets both spouses' needs at the same time. **Sometimes we just need to consider other options.**

OUR JOURNEY TO FINDING JOY IN MARRIAGE (AND THE THINGS WE LOST ALONG THE WAY)

We were in a diner eating pizza. The young couple sitting across the table from us had just asked us how we've sustained the joy of our relationship over the years. I wasn't exactly expecting that question, so my first answer was pretty simple: **we spend a lot of time together.** Talking, dreaming, laughing, debriefing. Companionship and intimacy require time, and lots of it.

When we were first married, we retreated together to cheap lawn chairs overlooking bushes that barely shielded us from the highway on the other side. We walked all over that university town, in all kinds of weather, for our date nights. We might walk to the library for a free movie and share an order of breadsticks from Papa John's, where even with the sauces, our meal totaled a mere $3.69.

Later we added children, and enough disposable income for Jonathan to buy me a porch swing. We'd sit in that thing and talk while our children played. At night, we'd tuck them into bed and sneak back out to talk some more, with hot chocolate or bug spray as our companions, depending on the weather.

Even after losing both the yard and the porch swing in our move to Cambodia, we found a way to escape together. We'd head up to our roof and sit in bamboo chairs (with bug spray as our definite companion), watch the city skyline, and share soul secrets. These days you'd be more likely to find us sipping coffee at our kitchen table, the kitchen door conveniently locked behind us.

But the more I pondered this young couple's question about joy in marriage, and the more I traced our marital history over the years, the more I realized that finding joy was about losing things too. On the journey to find joy in marriage, we've shed some surprising baggage.

Who's in charge here??

I went into marriage spouting ideals of male headship. My husband

Jonathan would be in charge and make the final decisions, and I, as the wife, would submit. In any disagreement, his opinion would count for more. We thought we believed that premise, and because we didn't have a lot of conflict, we thought we were pretty good at following it.

In real life, however, I don't think we ever actually *practiced* male headship (or what is sometimes called complementarianism, a term I didn't know at the time). We thought we did, because we loved God and wanted to obey His Word. And male headship is what the Bible instructs, right??

But Jonathan never pulled the "I'm in charge" card on me. Never. Not even once. Not even when he felt led overseas and I didn't. I put pressure on myself to submit to his call, but it never came from him.

A little premarital advice from my mom

Growing up, I watched my mom honoring her husband, and she taught me to do the same. When it came to practical advice, though, she focused on "talking things out." She told me that in her marriage to my dad, if one of them cared about something more — whoever it was — they went with that. The next time it might be different, and that was ok, because nobody was keeping track. She said if they didn't agree, they just kept talking until they did agree. **Practically speaking, my mom and dad were on equal terms in their marriage.**

One day my mom told me about a conversation with some other Army wives. One of the women turned to my mom and told her that *she must really love her husband.* Mom was a bit confused; she hadn't been raving about how wonderful Dad was or how much she loved him. But something in the way she talked about him (or *not* talked about him, as the case may have been) spoke her love loud and clear to those fellow Army wives.

Now I know that the type of marriage my mom was describing follows the mutual submission outlined in Ephesians 5:21: *Submit to one another out of reverence for Christ.* Now I know that people call this type of relationship "egalitarian." But it's almost as if back then, we

22

had no vocabulary for the Biblical marriage conversation.

The priesthood of all believers

Even in the early days of our marriage, whenever we needed to make a big decision, Jonathan and I would always pray together. We assumed that God would impress the same thing on our hearts, and that we would be united in both seeking God and obeying Him.

Looking back now, I can see that the path to egalitarianism begins with the priesthood of all believers. We went into marriage saying we believed in male headship, yet in decision-making, we fully expected God to speak to both of us. We believed we could, and would, both hear from God, and that God would say the same thing to both of us. Blame it on the *Experiencing God* craze of the 1990's if you want, but this is how we approached God from the very beginning of our marriage.

Love and Respect??

Several years into our marriage I heard about the idea of "love and respect," which claims that a woman's biggest need is to be loved by her husband and that a man's biggest need is to be respected by his wife. That seemed like good, solid, Biblical advice. In our marriage I felt loved, my husband felt respected, and we were happy. "Hmm," I thought, "love and respect must be the key to marital happiness."

Then I read a book about the idea (the book is long for being built on the foundation of only one verse). About halfway through, I had to put it down. It was so tedious I couldn't finish it. How many more stories and examples could there be?? The book seemed to be repeating itself.

Besides, I felt like something was missing. I need my thoughts, ideas, and intellect valued: I need respect. Almost as much as love. And my husband needs love, perhaps more than respect. He can't survive without my compassion, empathy, and listening ears.

(In all fairness to the author of these ideas, he has elsewhere stated that men and women need both love and respect, though in differing amounts. It's just that I

didn't get that impression from reading his book or from watching his videos.)

Lest you get the wrong idea here, let me make one thing clear: I deeply respect my husband. I value his opinions and consult him on everything. I turn to him for counsel, guidance, and perspective. I trust his advice and regularly defer to him in decision-making. He most certainly has my respect.

But for him, although my respect is nice, if I did not also care about his feelings, his dreams, and his deepest longings, and if I did not tenderly take care of him, he would shrivel up and die (his words, not mine). He needs my open-hearted love. And if he loved and cared for my deepest hurts and feelings, but did not also value my gifts and abilities, I'd be crushed. **In fact, if I didn't have his respect, I wouldn't actually feel loved by him.**

Receiving only love or only respect isn't good enough for Jonathan and me. We need both love *and* respect. The teaching of "Love and Respect" was a nice start, but for us, it didn't go far enough. As a wife, yes, I respect my husband, and as a husband, yes, Jonathan loves his wife. It's in the Bible; it's good. But God isn't going to be offended if wives also love their husbands, and husbands also respect their wives.

In the book of Ephesians, Paul was improving upon the pagan hierarchies of the day (See *Paul, the Misogynist?* by Elizabeth). Neither Paul nor Jesus – who demonstrated both love and respect for women *repeatedly* in the Gospels – is going to be upset if we take these instructions that much further, if we add more love and respect, and more *imago dei (the belief that our Creator made us in His image, and that we have inherent value and worth)*, to our relationships. On the contrary, I think it pleases Him.

"A marriage where either partner cannot love or respect the other can hardly be agreeable, to either party." — Jane Bennett in Pride and Prejudice *(Sorry, just had to get my Austen on for a minute.)*

Encountering Jesus as healer

The more I considered this young couple's question, the more I kept coming back to the same answer: emotional healing. Emotional healing is what happens when Jesus walks into our pain and binds up the wounds of our hearts. Emotional healing is what draws us closer to each other than ever before.

It's what enables us to answer Karen Carpenter's velvet-voiced, pain-tinged question: "Why do we go on hurting each other, making each other cry, hurting each other, without ever knowing why?" Emotional healing shows us both *why* we hurt each other and also, how to *stop* hurting each other.

Pursuing emotional wholeness is a journey Jonathan and I have been on for four years now. And though we walk together, our paths look different. The healing Jonathan needed came in the form of expressing long-hidden grief. For me, it meant beginning to feel long-hidden feelings.

For both of us, the path to healing has trodden straight through pain, but it's been worth it, for the healing we've found has deepened our intimacy and intensified our joy.

Perhaps the honeymoon should have worn off by now, but it hasn't. We have more joy and intimacy after 15 years of the "daily grind" than we ever dreamed possible.

Along the way, we've shed strict interpretations of gender roles and lost deep emotional wounds. In their place, we've welcomed emotional healing and embraced mutual love and respect.

We are co-heirs with Christ and co-leaders in our home. We lead each other closer to Jesus, closer to love, closer to wholeness. We give each other space to grow, and we say the hard truth to each other, too.

This is what our Joy looks like.

I'M A PROVERBS 31 FAILURE

"A wife of noble character, who can find?"

Recently, as my husband read aloud from Proverbs 31 over the breakfast table, I wondered if maybe that was a rhetorical question. As in, "can *anyone* find this woman?" She has an extensive list of accomplishments and abilities. She seems to be able to "do it all," with skill. Am I really supposed to be like her?

I have this vague notion that the modern Proverbs 31 woman stays at home with her (many!) children, educates them at home, makes all their (organic!) meals from scratch, enthusiastically serves her church community, and, after all that, is still (frequently!) romantically available to her husband. And while there is certainly nothing wrong with any of these endeavors individually, I personally cannot live up to all these expectations at once.

Thankfully, my husband has a firm belief that "nobody does it all." "Something always gets dropped," he often tells me. He believes this because he watched his mom *choose* not to "do it all." He was never under the impression that one woman could — or should — do it all. His mom did stay at home with her eight children, and homeschool them, but she was not involved in church ministry, nor did she have a home business. The meals she prepared for her family were exceedingly simple. Sometimes it was cereal for supper. Other times it was baked potatoes, with nothing but cottage cheese as a topping. Her home, however, was a place of joy and peace that others felt drawn to.

(Incidentally, when my husband closed the Bible that morning, he sighed, "I don't think this woman exists. And if she did, I don't think I'd like her.")

I have never been one of those women who could juggle several responsibilities at once. In college, I took a mere 12 or 13 hours each semester. With the remainder of my time, I tended to my marriage, and together, we volunteered at our church. A couple of times, I tried to extend my summer job into the school year. Each time the attempt ended with me quitting that job.

I recently had an opportunity to admit to myself yet again that I cannot do it all (and retain some semblance of sanity). I decided I should study Khmer during my short summer break. It was so hard, I about had a breakdown. Or . . . maybe I did have a breakdown. Ask my husband. On second thought, don't ask him! It was he who suggested I quit studying, after noticing that I had absolutely no energy left over for the family. I was adamant that I continue – because a missionary wife *should* know the local language. It's, like, a requirement or something.

I know so many missionary wives who *do* speak Khmer well, and I thought I was such a failure not to be like them. But if I am to listen to my husband's wisdom, I must accept that I can't do it all. I must drop something. And at this point in my life, I am choosing to drop further language learning. I've got five people in my family who need me – to laugh at their jokes, to care for their troubles, and to be engaged with what's happening from day to day. I couldn't do that when I was studying language.

Truth be told, language learning is not the only thing I have dropped. I've also dropped ministry outside my home. I used to be active in ministry with my husband, and I loved it. Right now, though, the focus of my ministry is my home – my husband and children. But the truth of the matter is also that homeschooling all day pretty much takes everything I have to give. I need the help of a lady to do basic cleaning tasks each day, and to cook our noon meal. I have clearly failed in this whole womanhood thing. I mean, wives should cook, and stuff. Right?

But, if I hadn't dropped the cooking and cleaning, I would have been forced to drop other things. Things I didn't want to drop. Like adequate school time for my children. And adequate sleep for me (perhaps transforming me into the classic Proverbs 31 woman who wakens early and works late into the night??).

My husband doesn't want me *plus* language fluency. He just wants me. My children don't want me *plus* gourmet meals. They just want me. My friends don't want me *plus* a clean house. They just want me.

The best way for me to stay *me* is not to pretend I do it all and do it all well. Because I don't. And I can't. I very deliberately drop many things in my life, so that I may whole-heartedly embrace the things I haven't dropped.
I don't get it all done. I am a Proverbs 31 failure. But my family gets a happier me. A nicer me. A more likeable me.

If I didn't fail as a Proverbs 31 woman, I am convinced I would be far less successful at loving people. The greatest command of all.

WHAT I WANT TO TEACH MY DAUGHTERS ABOUT MARRIED SEX

I've been married for 17 years now. While that's not as long as some of you — and certainly not as long as my husband's grandparents' 70 years — it's still long enough to have seen and heard a lot of marriage advice.

And you know what? Some of that advice makes me cringe. **So I can tell you up front: I'm not going to advise you to make sure to meet your husband's needs by having lots of sex with him.** And I'm not going to tell you that the purpose of marriage is to make you holy. *(It isn't.)*

What I *do* want to talk about is walking in sexual wholeness.

How can I possibly talk about a topic as big and complex as human sexuality in a single blog post? While I can't offer the comprehensiveness or the nuance that a book or a therapist can offer, I'll give you my basic framework.

These are the things I want to teach my daughters someday: what the foundation for healthy married sexuality is, potential obstacles in the bedroom and what to do about them, and potential temptations outside of marriage and what to do about them.

1) The Philosophy of Nakedness

I believe Nakedness is the foundation for healthy married sexuality. Remember how Adam and Eve were naked in the garden and not ashamed? Yes that was before sin, and yes now we live as sinners in a sinful world, but their unashamedness in marriage? It's still possible.

And yet. It's not the nakedness itself that's so key; it's what the nakedness represents.

Nakedness isn't about taking off your clothes just for the sake of taking off your clothes (although that's helpful). Nakedness is about

29

much more than that. It's about being comfortable in your body, just the way it is right now. It's about being with your husband, with the lights on and your clothes off.

(Practical note: this is why locks and curtains are so important.)

Nakedness is about loving the body God formed in you and declared *good*. It's about delighting in all your cells, including the ones that bring pleasure — and yes, even including the ones that don't look "picture perfect." It's about being with the one you love, fully accepted and fully at home.

It's about skin touching skin and souls sharing secrets between the sheets: being seen, being <u>known</u>, being loved, ALL of you, and all of me. It's about the tremendous trust it takes to let go and let someone see your wilder side without fear of rejection or disapproval.

This kind of Nakedness goes beyond the "frequency fights" many couples have and speaks to the tenor of your relationship when you *are* together. Is it easy-going and uninhibited, characterized by affection, acceptance, and trust? Because that's what Eden feels like, and what we all long for.

But... what if Nakedness isn't easy?

2) What to do when Nakedness is hard

It's no casual matter to search for this kind of open-hearted, unembarrassed nakedness. You can't just throw off your clothes in a desperate attempt to grasp at this intimacy. **If you're new to marriage, or if your marriage is wounded, remember that getting Naked may be a slow journey, and there may be obstacles in the way.**

You may feel shame about your body. You may have long-standing body hatred or even struggle with some accompanying <u>disordered eating</u>. You may have suffered abuse before or feel shame over your sexual past. You may even bear physical or emotional pain from your marriage itself.

Or maybe it's your husband who's struggling. Maybe he's looking at pornography, dealing with sexual addiction, or reeling from abuse of his own.

We carry our wounds and insecurities, our body image issues and porn addictions, with us into marriage. They don't magically go away when we say our vows and put on a sparkling ring. We carry our whole selves into our bedrooms; we're not separate people there. We may lock the door behind us, but it's not a strong enough door to keep out the rest of our soul and spirit.

Some of the things I've mentioned are deep, deep spiritual issues. And while they don't necessarily start in the bedroom, they do show up there and, sadly, they won't go away on their own. They often require extra care and help. So could I gently suggest you seek some outside help? You may need to reach out to a qualified counselor for some of the psychological and emotional issues. You may need to seek medical care if you're experiencing physical pain or wonder if your hormones are out of balance.

The unfortunate catch, of course, is that finding a good counselor or medical doctor may prove difficult if you're living overseas. You may need to do these things on a visit to your passport country or in a neighboring country for respite, or consider talking to someone on Skype. I want to give you permission to think about, pray for, and plan a time to get some outside help.

If you struggle with marital intimacy, that there is no shame in it. My husband and I dealt with several of these issues, including body hatred, disordered eating, past sexual abuse, and guilt over choices we made before marriage. **Whatever your particular struggle, do not be ashamed, and remember: you are not alone.**

3) When temptation comes my way

Finally, I want to talk about what happens when our sexual energy starts unfolding in the wrong direction — that is, *away* from our husbands. **What happens when you find yourself attracted to**

another man? (Because yes, this happens to married people, and it's happened to me before.)

My husband once infamously wrote that, as a way of protecting our marriage, he tells me when he feels attraction to another woman. We didn't expect to receive so many private emails asking us how exactly that works in our marriage. How are we able to trust each other like that? While the full answer to that question is outside the scope of this post, it brings up an important topic: how *can* we deal with temptation?

Part of the answer lies in the understanding that sexual desire is more than physical attraction. (I mean, it's also physical attraction; otherwise what's all that Naked Time for?) But sexual desire is also emotional and intellectual attraction. It's being interested in the things a person is talking and thinking about. It's being paid the ultimate compliment of attention to *your* thoughts and feelings.

People think temptation comes in pretty little packages, but it doesn't have to. Certainly temptation may be physical, but more often I believe it's metaphysical. And if we want to take our marriage vows seriously (and we *do*), we've got to be aware of the spiritual and emotional side of attraction.

But here's the good news: we can use this aspect of attraction to our advantage. We don't have to let it lead us away from our husbands. We can let it lead us *to* our husbands. So pay attention to what interests you. Pay attention to the kinds of things you find yourself talking about with other people.

And those things you find interesting to talk about with other people, talk about with your husband. The things you find fun to do and to watch and to laugh about, laugh about and do with your husband. Take your desires home to him.

Then dig in deeper. Go beyond talking about the kids, ministry or work (although some of that is fine and good and healthy). Ask about his childhood and what formed him. Ask about his dreams and tell him yours. Talk about how you fell in love. Talk about what you love about God. Talk about how God is talking to you and how He's *not* talking to you.

Lastly, remember to be guarded around any man with whom you feel that special spark of connection.

~~~~~~~~~~~~~~~~~~

Thus ends my Big Picture understanding of married sexuality.

I believe in getting naked, body and soul.

I believe in getting outside help when we can't find the kind of Edenic intimacy we all desire.

And I believe in protecting our marriages from temptation, body and soul.

I believe sex is more spiritual than we usually like to think.*

And I believe that spiritual component is vital in making marital sexuality flourish.

May you and your husband experience the raw joy of knowing and being known. May you know the thrill of intimacy between the sheets and between hearts. And may your souls and your bodies grow into and around each other as you spend your days and your lives together.

WHAT CHRISTIANS CAN LEARN FROM A NEW YORK TIMES ARTICLE ABOUT SLEEPING WITH MARRIED MEN

The *New York Times* recently published an article by Karin Jones entitled, "What Sleeping With Married Men Taught Me About Infidelity." A friend shared it, and I read it. I found I had a lot to say about it, so I commented on my friend's Facebook share, where it received so much positive feedback that I thought I'd share it here. But my response will make more sense if you take the time to read the article first.

My worldview obviously differs from the author's – in fact I might say it diverges greatly – but I think she makes some important observations. My thoughts on this subject are influenced, of course, by nearly 18 years of marriage. But they are also greatly informed by my husband's readings on relationships and sex.

Before you think that sounds too weird, let me explain why he reads extensively about these issues: he works with a lot of couples in his pastoral counseling ministry. For the record, I don't know who any of his clients are; I only know about the ideas in his books. (The only exception to this would be when a client of his walks up to me and announces, "Your husband is my counselor." This is not frequent but has occasionally been known to happen.)

And now that I've finished all my caveats, we can move on to my thoughts about the *New York Times* article.

~~~~~~~~~~~~~~~~~~~~~~~~~~~~~

I know it might sound crazy to say this, but I think a lot of "Christian" wisdom is not super helpful to marriage and that we can learn from "secular" or research-based sources. First off, sex is more important to a marriage than we in Christian circles sometimes like to think. Dr. Barry McCarthy, author of the 2015 book *Sex Made Simple: Clinical Strategies for Sexual Issues in Therapy*, claims that a counselor simply cannot afford to treat only the communication/relationship aspect of a marriage and assume good sex will follow.

Rather, McCarthy claims, sex must be addressed separately and intentionally, in addition to other relationship needs. Sex is too important to the marriage for a counselor to be silent on the issue. And it's highly complex and individual. This is part of the reason it needs purposeful addressing, though even many counselors are uncomfortable talking about it.

The research shows that couples in America are having less and less sex, with a good percentage (around 15%) being in what is considered a "sexless marriage" (sex 10 times a year or less). The research also shows that when a couple stops having sex, it's more often the husband's decision, not the wife's (this information was also found in McCarthy's book, where he quotes H. Feldman's 1994 article in the *Journal of Urology*).

The fact that sexlessness was primarily dependent on the man was news to me as women often get slandered in culture for being "frigid." This mischaracterization seems key to common "Christian" teaching that women want affection and connection, while men want sex. Research shows that this traditional approach is unhelpful in the sexual arena: women want good sex too. This is something the author of the *New York Times* article touched on and something proponents of the traditional view often neglect. God made us all sexual beings, and satisfying sex is important for both spouses in a marriage.

Another aspect of relationships that the article's author noted was that men do not just want sex. They want connection and affection as well. Maybe it's modern American culture, or maybe it's American "Christian" culture, or maybe it's both, but men are sometimes expected to be emotionless and connectionless in favor of more "manly" behavior.

If you want support for that claim, you can listen to this radio program about the way men's human needs are marginalized in modern American culture. I think the church needs to push back against this aspect of mainstream culture and show a better way — one based in our foundational beliefs of a relational Godhead and of humans created in God's image. The Bible is actually good news for culture, even when culture accuses it of being otherwise.

This artificial differentiation between men's needs and women's needs is unhelpful for marriage and society in general. Men are images of God as well as women, and God is a relational God. Men and women both want loving, secure attachments, and men and women both want satisfying sex. I wish we didn't have some of these stereotypes, stereotypes I learned before marriage as important for maintaining a happy marriage: a man should give his wife the affection she so desires, so that she will be more willing to give him the sex he so desires.

(In my mind this teaching is parallel to the teaching that women only need love and men need respect, which I believe is categorically untrue. Both men and women need both love and respect, and behaving otherwise treats human beings as too one-dimensional and cheats them both of intimacy and relational fulfillment. But I digress.)

The Bible does not even support this idea of "his needs, her needs" or "women give sex to get love and men give love to get sex." The woman in *Song of Solomon* showed strong sexual desire and initiation. Paul, often accused of being misogynistic (though I no longer think he was), told married couples that sex goes both ways — the wife's body belongs to her husband, and the husband's body belongs to his wife's. Meaning: the woman has desire too. Men aren't the only ones who want sex. **It seems to me that sex is actually a place in marriage where our theology gets worked out, but we rarely think about it that way.**

I do appreciate the author's note that even the urge to have an affair could be the beginning of an important conversation in marriage. Of course we as Christians believe this: temptation does not inevitably lead to sin. Temptation can be a wake-up moment and lead to increased marital intimacy, but only if we, like the author suggests, are willing to be honest with ourselves and with our spouses.

If we desire something we are not currently experiencing, we need to talk to our spouses about it, and not (if the Bible is our authority) seek out extramarital affairs. Research from the Gottman Institute indicates that being able to talk about sexual issues is essential to sexual satisfaction: "Only 9% of couples who can't comfortably talk about sex with one another say that they're satisfied sexually."

Meaning: if you can't talk about sex with each other, the likelihood that you're having mutually satisfying sex is pretty low. But, like Jones explains in her article, talking about sex can be risky. You might find out something about yourself that you don't want to know. You might feel rejected. And that was apparently too high a risk for the married men she was sleeping with.

Esther Perel, who is referenced in the article, has a fascinating TED talk on the interplay and tension between love and desire. I've actually watched it several times as I believe its vocabulary is helpful. It may not be specifically Christian teaching, but there is nothing anti-biblical about it. It frames the monogamy conversation better than it has sometimes been framed, and I encourage you to watch it (TED talks are, after all, fairly short).

The Bible seems to indicate that the intimacy — including sexual intimacy — that we can experience in marriage is only a small picture of God's love for us and what He intends for us to experience with Him for all eternity. So it only makes sense that Satan would attack our sexuality as it is intended to be lived out, both before marriage and in marriage.

Our cultures are obsessed with sex, but according to research, few people are actually having mutually emotionally and physically satisfying sex. So the ways we as a culture are seeking sexual fulfillment are not working. We're seeking it in all the wrong ways.

Sometimes because terrible things have been done to us, sometimes because we have simply believed the culture's (Satan's) lies. There are a myriad of reasons our sexuality gets broken in this world.

If we care about our own marriages and the marriages of our children, if we care about the marriages in the future Church, sex cannot be some taboo topic that we think will work itself out in silence. It won't. It needs specific cultivating and sometimes outside help (in the form or medication or therapy), and there is absolutely no shame in seeking help and wholeness for a part of our lives that is not thriving.

But if we feel ashamed of needing help, we won't seek it. So if this article can do any good in the world, I hope it can empower people in marriage whose sex life is less than they desire, to seek out help somewhere. I believe seeking healing is worth it.

References:

What Sleeping With Married Men Taught Me About Infidelity, by Karin Jones for *New York Times*.

The Secret to Desire in a Long-Term Relationship, a 20-minute TED talk by Esther Perel

Sex Made Simple: Clinical Strategies for Sexual Issues in Therapy, by Barry McCarthy.

Couples That Talk About Sex Have Better Sex, by Kyle Benson for the Gottman Institute, *https://www.gottman.com/blog/couples-talk-sex-better-sex/*

How American Masculinity Creates Lonely Men, a 48-minute program by Shankar Vedantam for NPR

From Jonathan: On Making Love,
https://trotters41.com/2017/11/25/on-making-love/

Other articles Jonathan and I have written about sex and marriage,
https://trotters41.com/2017/07/21/17-years-of-marriage-and-this-is-all-weve-got/

INTENSITY AND INTENTIONALITY {A NOTE ABOUT MARRIAGE AND MOTHERHOOD ON THE FIELD}

A while back our organization asked me to write a little something about marriage and motherhood on the field. At the time I wasn't sure whether I wanted the article to be anonymous or not, as I obliquely discuss both my children and my marriage in it. So I waited awhile before deciding (with both Jonathan's and my children's approval) that this is something that I could share publicly.

~~~~~~~~~~~~~~~~~~~~~~~~~~~~~~~~~~~~~~~

Two words come to mind when I think about marriage and motherhood on the field: Intensity and Intention. After living internationally for over four years, my experience has been that everything about living overseas is more intense than living in your passport country.

It's more physically intense. It's wildly hot where I am, with no central air conditioning. Housework takes longer as there are fewer automated devices. Electricity and water are sometimes unreliable, and food and water supplies aren't as clean. That meant that in the beginning especially, we were ill more often – and more severely – than we were back "home." Life in another country is also more mentally and emotionally intense. Learning a strange, new culture and doing everything in a new language is hard work. You make mistakes and misunderstand things every day.

Anyone crossing cultures must deal with these changes and stressors, but as a parent, I also bear witness to the strain of crossing cultures on my children. They get annoyed by aspects of life here: it's loud, it's crowded, and we have no yard or playgrounds nearby. They don't like the way local people touch them or stare at them, and they don't particularly like the local cuisine (or at least, not all of it). Life here is transitory, and the friends they make often move in and out of their lives with little advance warning. On top of all that, they miss friends and family back home – especially grandparents.

In light of the intensity of missionary life, I have to be more intentional about marriage and motherhood. I need to care for my children's hearts in a way I wouldn't if we lived in America. Of course we have the same pre-school and pre-adolescent emotional turmoil that children and parents have in their home culture, but we also have more potential issues. I have to keep my own heart soft towards my kids, and I need to take the time to validate their feelings. This is difficult to do as I am already emotionally, physically, and spiritually stretched to the max myself. Practically speaking, it means I also need to carve time out of our schedule so they can communicate with friends and family back home (usually that's through Skype).

Marriage is the same way: I have to be intentional about taking care of it. Simply surviving here takes more time and energy, so it's tempting not to spend enough time on my marriage. But of course when I don't spend time on it, my marriage suffers. The less time I spend on my marriage, the farther I drift away from my husband, and the harder it is to bring us back to together again. Likewise, the more time and effort I pour into my marriage, the easier and more fulfilling it is. It becomes life-giving instead of life-draining, as it does when I'm not nurturing it enough.

In order to pour so much time and energy into my husband and my children, I have to be intentional about filling myself up. I have to be vigilant about taking care of my spirit by getting up early to spend time with God. I have to be diligent about taking care of my mind and body by eating at regular intervals throughout the day, exercising four or five days a week, and going to bed on time. If I don't do these things, I don't have enough emotional energy to pour into my husband and children, who need me so much.

In many ways marriage and parenting on the field is the same as it is in my home culture, but its intensity level is higher. Missionary life simply requires more of me, and in order to match its intensity, I have to be intentional about taking care of both myself and my family. I have to daily turn my heart toward them and toward God. When I don't, the consequences are great. But when I do, the reward is greater still.

A few years ago I wrote a series (at alifeoverseas.com) on life in ministry families and the thinking patterns we absorb along the way. As I mentioned then, this conversation is for everyone — whether you grew up as a Pastor's Kid (PK) or Missionary Kid (MK), whether you entered ministry as an adult, or whether you love people who are.

This article discusses three of the lies Timothy Sanford writes about in his book, *I Have to be Perfect, and other Parsonage Heresies.* As we process these statements, keep in mind that everybody experiences life differently. You might react to some of these ideas and not to others, and that's ok.

"I'm here for others" & "Other people's needs are more important than my own"

Ouch. These two lies hit close to home for me. They're so intertwined that they're hard to separate, and I've believed them both as a ministry wife. I've assumed people can walk all over me. All over my time, and all over my feelings. I've allowed people to trash my home, believing I must silently endure it as service to Christ. I've bought into the lie that I exist only to serve others, and that I can't have needs of my own. Furthermore, **I thought if I didn't let other people do those things to me — and even more specifically, if I weren't joyful about it — then I wasn't a good Christian or a good ministry wife.**

I required these things of myself. Did God require them of me? Must I only ever serve others? Philippians 2:4 tells us to "look not only to our own interests, but also to the interests of others." That's an intriguing grammatical construction, the "not only, but also." The Apostle Paul, arguably the greatest missionary of all time, seems to be assuming that we have needs of our own and simply encourages us to care for others in addition to ourselves.

Galatians 6:2 instructs us to "Bear one another's burdens." Other versions say to "share" or "carry" one another's burdens. I have a hard time deciding which verb I like best, so let's use all of them: we are to bear, share, and carry one another's burdens. **The words "one another" imply a reciprocal relationship: I help to carry your burdens, and you help to carry mine.**

We're accustomed to carrying other people through *their* difficult times. We're not "supposed" to have troubles of our own. We're not supposed to need someone to carry us; instead we need to keep carrying other people. But what about those times when we can no longer carry someone else? What about the times we can't even carry ourselves? Can we let someone carry us for a change?

Being in ministry or missions doesn't mean we'll never need to be carried. It doesn't mean we'll never have needs. Sometimes we get comfortable stuffing our needs down and ignoring what our souls are saying to us. Sometimes we get accustomed to giving when we have nothing left to give. And sometimes we model those behaviors in our families.

Maybe we can start to acknowledge that we have needs of our own. Maybe we can allow others to pour into us for a time. Maybe we can give ourselves a little bit of the grace we offer so freely to others. (The flip side of this, of course, is that other people have to be willing to care for us, too.)

What does it take to create a community characterized by Galatians 6:2, a community of mutual burden-bearers who help each other through the troubles of life? It takes an acceptance, *by all of us,* that we don't always have to be strong. It's ok to be weak. It's ok to depend on others, even if we're in ministry — perhaps *especially* if we're in ministry.

The idea that "other people's needs are more important than my own" sounds very spiritual. It sounds very sacrificial and giving. But we are all of us humans, created and finite beings with limited resources. Our lives are powered by the Holy Spirit, true, but **none of us can survive if we think we are *only* here for others, or if other's needs are always more important than our own.**

43

There's a deeper, more insidious lie at work here, too. **When we believe the lie that the only purpose of our life is to serve other people, we buy into the falsehood that we earn our worth.** That our performance justifies our existence. That what we do, the service we yield for others, is what makes us valuable in both God's eyes and other people's eyes.

We need to remember the Truth. We need to know, in the core of our being, **down in the cellar of our souls,** that God's love and approval do not depend on anything we do. The same God who made us from dust knows we are dust, and He redeemed us Himself. We are caught in His arms, caught in His gaze, and **there is nothing left for us to prove.** There is only God's love, and the Cross has already proved it.

"I should already know"
This lie claims that I should already be farther along in my spiritual journey that I am right now. That whatever I know, I *should* know more. That wherever I am, I *should* be farther along. That whatever my faith is, it *should* be stronger. That however my relationship with God is faring, it *should* be better.

And of course my own personal favorite, oft-uttered in frustration: "Arg!! I should be a better person by now!!"

So. Many. Shoulds.

Saying and believing *should* entraps us. I *should* be nicer to that person. I *should* forgive those people. What happened back then *shouldn't* still hurt. I *shouldn't* be so angry at God. I *should* be less selfish and more generous. I *should* be more mature. I *shouldn't* struggle with this sin anymore. I *shouldn't* struggle with the "little" hardships in my life. I *should* be happier.

There's nowhere to go but down to the depths of despair if I don't do what I *should* do. If I'm not living life the way I *should*, then I'm a bad person. If I'm not as good as I *should* be, I've failed in my faith. If

44

I'm not as dedicated as I *should* be, I've failed in my Bible study, failed in my prayer life, failed in my service to others.

Should looks to a past full of failures.

***Should* judges us as Insufficient! Inadequate! Unworthy!**

***Should*. This one single word oppresses us.**

What can we do about the crushing shoulds in our life?? Timothy Sanford suggests replacing them with coulds. Where *should* condemns, *could* gives hope. Where *should* breeds anxiety and fear, *could* sees opportunity for growth. Where *should* paralyzes, *could* expands. I *could* talk to God more. I *could* read His Word more. I *could* forgive that person. I *could* love that person more fully. **A life of *coulds* is full of possibilities.**

I want to give you permission to dump the *shoulds* in your life. I'd love to simply say the words and be confident that you're no longer captive to your own *shoulds*. But I know better — I know it takes more than just saying the words. I'm going to say them anyway: **You don't need to do more or be better than you are right now.** You are already Enough.

Wherever you are in your walk is acceptable for today. You're right where you're supposed to be. Every day you'll grow. Every day you'll be farther along than you were the day before, even if you don't feel the change. **Every day you'll receive another dose of Grace, the medicine settling deeper into your soul.**

The beauty, the mystery of it all, is that Grace happens without any *shoulds* at all. **So let us release ourselves from the tyranny of the *shoulds*.** Let us release our pastors from the *shoulds*. Let us release our missionaries. And for goodness sake, let us release their children. As people loved by a holy God and saved by Grace alone, let us rid ourselves of these lies before they imprint themselves onto the DNA of our souls.

Have you ever felt your needs didn't matter, or that you should already know or be a certain something?

In your life, do you think those beliefs came from within yourself, or externally from family culture or church culture, or some combination of the three?

Do you need to take some time to detox from these unspoken beliefs, to give yourself a time of solitude and silence in order to relinquish these pressures into the Father's hands?

The Homeschool Teacher Hat

Six Things I've Learned from Six Years of Homeschooling

Finishing a school year tends to put me in a reflective mood. And although this is not a homeschooling blog, homeschooling does take up a large portion of each day, so I reserve the right to write about it occasionally. Recently I've been thinking about some of the most important lessons I've learned about homeschooling, *for our family:*

1. I didn't need to homeschool preschool.

2. I needed co-op.

3. Every family, and every child, is different.

4. For me, homeschooling means staying at home.

5. I have to really want to homeschool.

6. I have to take regular breaks.

The starred items that appear in this blog post are ideas I heard from a video (as in VHS) series from my local library (yay!) called "How To Homeschool the Early Years." It was made in the late 90's (hey, I said it was VHS . . .) and was designed for parents of children ages 2 to 9. It was produced with the idea that not all parents are able to attend a homeschool conference, so the video series brought the conference to your home.

Ready? Ok, here goes! (Be forewarned, this is long. Those not interested in homeschooling might want to skip it!)

1) I didn't need to homeschool preschool.

This is one of the most practical and most freeing things I've learned about homeschooling. **Everything that must be done in Kindergarten – learning basic math facts and how to read – can be done in Kindergarten.** Other learning tasks, like colors, shapes, and sorting and stacking, happen naturally in family life, and you don't need a workbook for them. Truly, for children with lots of books, games, and siblings to play with, **preschool is redundant.**

Through their book *Better Late than Early*, homeschool pioneers Raymond and Dorothy Moore popularized the idea that a child's formal education needn't be rushed.* I didn't listen to that advice the first time around. I was eager to start homeschooling and didn't want my little four-year-old to fall behind in life (paranoid much?), so I started him on math and reading lessons.

Later I realized that was sort of pointless — and that the Moores were right. So with my second child, I didn't do anything specific for pre-school, other than have him listen to what I was reading aloud to my oldest. I did the same with my third, and plan to repeat that process with my fourth.

All you really need for preschool are some crayons and paper, a bunch of library books, and some developmental toys. While the library is free (I was virtually addicted to my public library in the States), toys and games require some money (sorry). Trotter preschoolers usually gravitate the most to magnets, pegs and pegboards, and Wedgits. I myself have been known to play with said toys for hours at a time, so I can attest to their enduring allure.

Another easy way to fill preschoolers' minds with stories and expose them to language is giving them books on tape/CD. (Bonus: Mom gets a break.) My kids still love listening to books on tape while they build their Lego "creations." I sometimes miss the simplicity of those early years, when all I did all day was nurse babies, read books with my children, and cook them meals. Now I have many more curriculum needs to balance.

2) I needed co-op.

As a young mom, I wasn't sure I wanted to homeschool. Someone recommended I join a co-op to learn more about it, so I did. The fellowship I found in co-op was invaluable. I met all these moms, and they were all so different, and none of them seemed to mind when I peppered them with questions and asked their advice. (Because really, who among us would pass up the opportunity to give advice when specifically asked??)

The co-op I participated in was fairly low-key, but it was perfect for me at that time in my life. It allowed me to get out of the house, which was a sanity saver, and gave my kids opportunities to play group games and take art, science, and cooking classes. It was also an ideal outlet for me to teach my favorite subjects — math and science — in a sometimes-mind-numbing season of motherhood.

I gained so much wisdom and perspective from experienced homeschool moms, even when my approach to school and family life was different from theirs. I collected their practical ideas and their curriculum recommendations, and I shuffled them over and over again in my mind as I researched the various homeschool methods and tried to decide what was best for our family.

Getting out of the house was so important for dealing with the intensity of small children in my home. Another way I did that was to attend the weekday Ladies' Bible Study that met at my church. Bible study broke up the monotony of life at home with littles. I learned so much from older Christian women, and they helped me through some very tough times — depression, death, infertility. I attended for years, and I remember those years fondly. *They were so good for my spiritual growth at a time when I really didn't know what I was doing with regard to faith and motherhood.*

3) Every family, and every child, is different.

Remember how I met all those moms through co-op? Well, they all homeschooled differently, and in the beginning, the educational options seemed overwhelming. Then I found *Cathy Duffy's 101 Top Picks for Homeschool Curriculum.* (I know. This sounds like an advertisement.)

The first half of the book (which is not curriculum reviews) walked me through all the steps to find my own style of education. She introduced the 6 major methods of home education, then she talked about learning styles. Next, she instructed parents to determine both your children's learning styles *and* your own learning style. This is because a parent's learning style will be his or her default teaching style, but it may not match the child's best learning style. (That was a major revelation for me.)

Then I went through the exercises to define my educational and family goals, which, in combination with the learning styles and teaching styles, helped me settle on the homeschool methods I use. Her book gave me clarity and confidence in my decisions, and it also helped me understand why there is so much diversity among homeschool families. Everybody is different, and **my homeschool won't look like yours, and that's ok**. It's actually good, because we're all doing what's best for our own families.

I also learned that each child might learn differently, and won't be able to learn the same way as a sibling does. What is easy for one child is not necessarily easy for another child – and that's ok. All children have harder subjects and easier subjects. They learn differently. I am here to be patient with their individual differences, but *I am also here to celebrate my child's strengths.*

{In case you're interested, I use a combination of approaches, which technically means I'm "eclectic." I order most of my materials from companies that use either a Charlotte Mason approach (Sonlight) or a Classical approach (Veritas Press). I also love Timberdoodle's hands-on learning products and have flirted with Montessori-type activities from time to time.}

4) For me, homeschooling means staying at home.

This might sound like it contradicts #2 and my love for co-op, but it's been my experience nonetheless. When my children were younger, I needed to get out of the house and find some camaraderie with other moms. But as my children have grown, so have their educational demands. There is more to do now, and I simply can't afford time out of the house on a weekly basis.

I once heard Monte and Karey Swan talk about homeschooling, and Karey's statements especially stayed with me.* They had pulled their kids out of the public school system so they could be more intentional in their discipleship and also so they could "move into creativity" as she called it (they were a very creative family). But then they found themselves driving all over town for co-ops, athletic practices, and music lessons. They didn't have the time to do all the things she really wanted to do.

Suddenly Karey realized she was "carschooling" instead of homeschooling, and their homeschool activity choices were defeating the purpose for which they removed their children from school. She wanted to be at home more, so they could move into creativity, so they could read together more, so they could have those deep discussions with their all-too-quickly-maturing children. So they quit the outside activities and centered their life around the home, and their family thrived in that environment. Monte and Karey's gentle approach to parenting appealed to me, and their story stuck with me.

Later I would experience a version of their story myself. In our first year overseas, I didn't know many homeschooling families, and our kids didn't have many friends. So I started a co-op with some other moms, and at the time, it was such a blessing to meet other homeschool moms in Phnom Penh and to watch my children form friendships with other kids. But after about six months of co-op, our gatherings no longer met the needs of *any* of the families. So we disbanded.

Our co-op was a success, though, because I'm still friends with those moms, and my kids are still friends with those kids. However, as my kids grew up more, their schoolwork started to pile up more too, and we couldn't make weekly or bi-weekly commitments anymore.

It's not just our educational needs that keep us mostly at home; it's also our emotional needs. We are a family of introverts. Both my husband and I are introverts, and all my children have some introverted qualities. That means that a week of getting out of the house every day or almost every day will wear.them.out. My kids will get cranky, and they won't even understand why they don't feel good. Too many outings mean I'll be too exhausted to read aloud to them for fun, or play games with them. I'll be too tired to connect with my husband on a deep level.

Every day, my children need time in their rooms to simply play, quietly and alone. They need that downtime to be able to concentrate properly on their schoolwork, and we give it to them on a regular basis. Their Mommy needs to be at home, too. I like to write, I like to play the piano, I like to exercise. None of those things gets done when we are scurrying to and from activities, no matter how good those activities are. Mostly staying at home is best for all of us.

5) I have to really want to homeschool.

When I was first exploring the idea of homeschooling our children, a woman at church told me very matter-of-factly that in order to homeschool, the mom has to really want to. She told me how her husband had wanted them to homeschool. She wasn't opposed to it and thought she would try it out for him, but she just wasn't all that interested in it. She was the one who had to do the teaching, not her husband, who had originally wanted it. Eventually, they quit, but it wasn't the end of the world. They just sent their kids to school, and mommy was happier.

I tucked that piece of advice away, and when I was researching homeschooling, I would bring it out from time to time and examine it. If this was going to work, if I were going to teach my kids day after day, month after month, year after year, I knew *I* needed to be the one in the family with the passion and drive for homeschooling. In the end I did develop that drive and that desire, even though it hadn't been there to begin with. I didn't think I could like homeschooling, but I do. (I didn't think I could like living overseas, either, but I do — can someone please tell me why this keeps happening to me???)

Of course, that's just my story. **It's ok if you don't want to homeschool. There is no one-size-fits-all family education plan. Every family is different (see #3 above), and every family makes decisions differently**. When I say, "I have to really want to homeschool," I don't say it in a we-just-have-to-force-ourselves-to-like-it kind of way. Rather, I mean that *for myself personally,* I need that desire in order to keep going.

If homeschooling is not your thing, that's totally ok. Homeschooling is just what our family does, and it works for us *at this point in time*. If you don't want to homeschool, or if you don't like it, then it just might not be a good fit for you. Everyone is different, so let's just move along and let everyone *be* different.

6) I have to take regular breaks.

If I'm going to teach my children at home for the long haul, I'm going to need endurance. And for me, one of the keys to endurance is pacing myself. I have to take daily breaks, decompress, and allow myself to think. I take an hour in the middle of the day to write – that's when I write emails and blog posts.

And I don't have an open door policy after bedtime. Once we say goodnight to our children, for the most part, they are not allowed out of their rooms. (Although there are exceptions to this rule.) Since I'm with them all day long, I need a breather in the evenings. Some moms might not require that; but I do. Evenings are for my husband and me to spend together.

I'm not the only one who needs breaks, though. My kids usually need a short break in between subjects, so I let them have that. That means that with 3 separate grade levels to juggle, in addition to short breaks in between subjects, and my "writing hour," our school day lasts all day. We are not done at lunchtime like some families, and that's ok. (It's also part of why we can't get out of the house too much.) We have a slower pace because in our family, hearts and minds work better that way.

Every quarter or so, we take a Thursday and Friday off. And we take a summer break. It's usually only four or five weeks because our school years are rather long. School years are long because we schedule a three-month furlough every other year; we have to take time off for third-world-country-sickness; and we host friends and family from the States at various times. Our summers are short, but I need them. **I am not mentally equipped to school year round**. Families who homeschool year-round make it sound relaxed and non-stressful. As wonderful as that sounds, I simply can't do it: I need my summer break!

TWO SANITY SAVING HOMESCHOOL PRACTICES

I've written lots of theoretical home schooling posts before, but sometimes we just need a little practical help. So that's what I've got for you today: two practices that are saving my sanity right now. Maybe they can help you, too.

LOOPS

I first heard of looping from Sarah Mackenzie (here and here). In a nutshell, loop scheduling is a technique that can be used for *subjects you need to get done regularly but that don't have to be completed every single day.* (That means math is a subject that should never be looped!) Classic looping examples come from the fine arts – things like picture study, composer study, and poetry reading. It can also be applied to various housework tasks.

When I first heard of looping, I didn't think the concept applied to me, so I ignored it and moved on. Then this year happened. I now have a 7th grader, a 5th grader, a 3rd grader, and a 1st grader. That's a lot of grade levels to manage. And it's a lot of language arts — if you, like me, think each child needs to do reading, spelling, phonics, handwriting, composition, grammar, and vocabulary each day.

The hours required to do that *many subjects within a subject* was eating up our days. And I constantly felt like a failure, as we simply could not finish every single piece of language study every day. Nobody had ever told me that all my children needed to do every language art every day, but somewhere along the way I internalized the expectation.

Then I started remembering my own middle school education. I only had language arts for one hour per day, plus homework. But that wouldn't add up to 3 or 4 hours per child per day (HALF our home school day), even in middle school. It would be 1 or 2, max.

Then I remembered some more: we studied language arts in *units*. We'd have a poetry unit, then a grammar unit, then a literature unit, then a composition unit. We didn't do all the things all at once.

I started thinking I needed to apply this to our home school. I started thinking in terms of units. If we're deep in an intensive writing unit that already takes a couple of hours a day, it's just torture to add the stress of separate spelling and grammar and vocabulary lessons at the same time. Why not finish the writing unit and then move on to the nitty-gritty of grammar or spelling?

And why had I not thought of this possibility before?

Later I spoke with my husband – who was himself homeschooled – about these things. He agreed that my expectations had been ridiculously high and supported my effort to find more reasonable expectations.

Then I spoke with my Home School Mom Friends, and they reminded me that my "new" approach had a name – it's called Looping.

So that's what we do now. We loop our language arts, and everybody is much happier and less stressed.

***We do not loop reading. Reading – both reading aloud together and reading silently alone — is the foundation of our education, and they happen every day. ***

LULLS

I'm a type-A, perfectionistic, over-achieving person with a bent towards workaholism. In the past, therefore, whenever we had any down time in the home school day (immediately after lunch, for example, or when all my kids were working on individual assignments), I tried to fill that time with other work: emails, blog posts, life planning, ministry event planning. I wanted to squeeze every available second out of my day.

This posed a problem for me, however, because in entering another world, I was drawn away from my home world. Once I entered the world of outside work, it was hard to shift my mind back into whatever school question (or sibling squabble question) was being asked. And an open computer is a distinct sign to children that you are not available to them.

My thoughts and attention ended up being divided, and I never felt like I finished any one thing. I was trying to become <u>more efficient</u> but ended up being *less* efficient. (Additionally there's the black hole of social media, surrounding which I deceive myself about how productive I'm really being.) I was perpetually exhausted in this kind of non-boundaried life. And I think my kids were getting less of me than they deserved.

So during school hours, I started committing not to open the computer in order to "be more efficient." I decided to read picture books to my youngest during that time. Or read something from my long list of books I'm always trying to get to but am too tired to read by the end of the day. When a child comes to you with a math question or a life question, it's much easier to put away a paper book than it is to put away a screen.

I call these times the Lulls. They are the lulls in the day that I used to try to fill with more work. Now I stay present and fill them with my own education or enjoyment, and I feel less harried. Before, I was always trying to rush through school work so I could get to my "other work." Now I don't rush. Now the school day is more peaceful. And it's all because I use my Lulls differently.

I should also mention that different days have different Lulls. If my older children are all doing a review assignment in math, I have much more Lull time. But if they each need to learn something new (or on the days we attend co-op), I have less Lull time. But that's OK. The Lull time isn't meant to be productive. I'm not trying to "get work done." I'm merely trying to be more focused and effective in filling the time gaps.

So here's how to apply the sanity-saving practices of Loops and Lulls to your day:

Loops: Follow those links up above to Sarah Mackenzie's Loop Scheduling instructions. Spend some time figuring out which of your subjects a) don't need to be done each day or b) already *aren't* getting done each day. Place them on a list and cycle through them one by one. All your looped subjects will now be getting done on a regular basis, and you'll feel less guilt and less pressure.

Lulls: Commit not to do other work while you're teaching your kids. This is hard, I know. We want to get as much done as possible each day — "redeem the time" and all that. But focusing on school work alone helps your day go much more smoothly and, in the end, helps you be more efficient and less stressed out.

Happy Home Educating!

PRACTICES THAT ARE REVOLUTIONIZING MY PARENTING

The speaker at church was encouraging us to look to God for mercy and healing, and then when God has healed you, to remember to thank Him. And suddenly I stopped, because I thought about all the things I've asked God for in the past, and I realized that I'm currently in a season where I'm living into some long-awaited dreams and receiving help for some long-asked-for requests.

Most of those prayers have to do with my parenting. I'm always praying to be a better mother — because I so often feel like a failure of a mother. Looking back that day, I started seeing that I *am* a different Mom than I used to be. And I'm a different wife. Not in every way and not in every moment, but I'm a person much more at peace in myself and in my circumstances. This is the fruition of long-awaited prayers.

The changes were slow and imperceptible, and I didn't even know it was happening at the time. I didn't even set out for it, I don't think. But I think I know some of the ways it was birthed. Many of the changes I'm going to talk about relate to homeschooling, but much of what I'm learning could probably apply to all parenting if you change some of the verbiage.

1. I started listening to different voices, and slowly I started thinking differently.

I used to keep up on a lot of post-fundamentalist news like the falls of Bill Gothard, Doug Phillips (of Vision Forum), and the oldest Duggar son. I was obsessed with needing to know, after having read a book on fundamentalist home school cults several years ago. I feared being part of the same "machine" that created these home school disasters. I got lost in cyberspace any time I had the chance. I would fall down an endless rabbit hole of meaningless blog posts and podcasts.

I don't do that anymore. Not that I don't occasionally get lost in cyberspace, but that I am much more selective with my influencers. I don't need knowledge of the most recent evangelical disasters in order to mother my children well, to nourish my own spiritual life, to connect with my husband, or to serve in local community. Instead I need encouragement and inspiration for the day at hand.

Now I listen to Sarah Mackenzie (of the Read Aloud Revival podcast (readaloudrevival.com) and the book *Teaching from Rest*, which continues to do its work on me), Brandy Vencel (of Afterthoughts blog {afterthoughtsblog.net} and the Schole Sisters podcast {scholesisters.com}, Cindy Rollins (of the Mason Jar podcast {circeinstitute.org/podcasts/the-mason-jar} and the book *Mere Motherhood*), and their influencers: the speakers and writers at the Circe Institute {circeinsttute.org} (my favorites are Angelina Stanford, Christopher Perrin, and Andrew Pudewa).

They've changed my thinking on education, its purpose, and its practical implications. They've stirred in me a hunger for discovery that I used to have, that got lost along the box-checking, high-performing, competitive way. They've inspired me to start reading poetry again.

And I listen to the artists and makers at the Rabbit Room {rabbitroom.com} (my favorites are Rebecca Reynolds and Andrew Peterson). They have pressed me further into the reality that I'm an image-bearer of God, and they've fortified my understanding of creativity and art. I've followed their lead in embracing the physical world, and as I've done so, I've become more fully human — and a more complete human makes a better mother.

2. I'm wrestling my perfectionism even more heartily than before.

It pops up in the unlikeliest of places, doesn't it? You think you've conquered it, but then you realize you are still drowning in lies. I was trapped in lies about what it meant to be a successful mother. I was trapped in lies about what it meant to send well-educated young people off into the world. I thought it had to be perfect. I thought there had to be zero educational gaps. I thought I had to prove *my* intellectual worth through my children's performance. That's a lot of pressure to live under.

I'm understanding more fully that we are not looking for perfection — in ourselves *or* our children. We're looking for progress. For growth. My husband likes to say, "All learning happens one step at a time." It's plastered on the wall of our home school, in fact. But though we had pounded that fact into our children's heads (with varying degrees of success), it had not yet reached down into mine.

I'm trying to put school in its proper place by giving it neither too much mental weight nor too little time. A bad day doesn't bother me as much anymore. (A bad week, yes. But a bad day or two, no.) So what if the math assignment bombed? So what if the writing assignment took half the day? We're not looking for perfection here, just steady work and steady improvement over time — and that means accepting setbacks with calm and patience.

Even if a child "loses it," I don't think the day is a bust. I know every day is a learning opportunity, and the days stack up to years, and there's always tomorrow to try again. I'm staying calmer and speaking more gently so I can look back at the end of a hard day with less dissatisfaction and fewer regrets. But I remember that even if I lose it, I can acknowledge it, seek forgiveness, and start again tomorrow.

[BONUS TIP: Their education *will* have holes. Yours does. Mine does. Everyone's does, no matter where or how their education took place.]

3. I've stopped putting my educational trust in curriculum.

I used to want to find a curriculum that was "perfect" (see the pattern here?). And I wanted that curriculum to basically *be* the teacher. I wanted to leave it alone and let my children become educated by it. I was saving my brain space for writing, you see. It was all about checking boxes so I could get away and get alone and fulfill my "real" calling.

But over and over again, I became frustrated by published resources. They're never exactly what I want, so I go looking elsewhere for perfection. It has taken me the greater part of 8 years to figure out that not only *can* I adapt a resource, but I *must*. I must tailor my children's education to them. They are individuals. I have to use my brain. I can't "save" it for later. I can't get lazy.

I have to engage with where my children are at that moment, both scholastically and emotionally. Where they are is the only place to begin, the only place to build from. And in truth, my children *are* my real calling. Not writing. They, and any human being placed in my path. [Note: this also explains why I publish much less frequently than I used to.]

How I teach now is much more akin to coaching or tutoring — which is always what I said I enjoyed more anyway. And it's much more satisfying. I see the struggle; I see the progress. I see the *child*. I've learned I don't even need curricula for some subjects – I can make them up myself (like writing), be a more hands-on teacher, and even get to experience the joy of better results. I'm leaning into these ways and gaining confidence that I *can* do these things. I don't have to trust a boxed curriculum.

[BONUS TIP: I had to stop thinking of my children en masse. They are not a herd. My family is a collection of individuals with differing temperaments and abilities. It's easy to think of children as a group when they're young, but as they grow, it becomes more and more important to see each child as an individual.]

4. I'm broadening my understanding of education.
I touched on this in #1, the voices I'm listening to. I used to put my children's education – or at least my contribution to it – in a box. Education equaled core work only. Education wasn't art or creativity or movement or theology or finances or health or real life. I didn't "do" real life. I did academics. But I'm realizing that these things are part of organic family life, part of all life.

If I'm engaged and not locked in a corner, I will naturally teach these things (alongside my husband who is already a natural teacher). I will encourage their creativity in art and architecture and storytelling. I will not think of these things as adjunct or auxiliary. They are central to becoming a fully *human* being. I don't need to be afraid that art or sports or relationship will steal from my children's robust-enough education. I can welcome them into our home and into our life.

5. I'm beginning to embrace assessment, and we've sought outside help for certain difficulties.

I used to despise standardized testing as I thought it unnecessarily stressed students out. And I still believe it does, for young students. But for older students, it can be a learning experience in which they learn how to take a test that can give some reassurance to both parent and child for work well done.

Separately, we reached a point with certain issues where we needed some outside perspective. Reaching out for help was the beginning of a journey to accept my children for who God created them to be, not who I imagined they would be. These assessments have given me the grace to accept my children as they are, while also gently stretching their capacities. And armed with new knowledge, I have better strategies for teaching my students.

The testing gave me the courage to take a long, hard look at myself and see my own difficulties reflected in my children. It allowed me to embrace differences between how I assumed my children would behave, and how they *actually* behave. It's helped me to better accept children who are the same as me as well as those who are different from me. And we have a lot more joy and connection.

6. I've purified the schedule, and I continually work to keep it that way.

As is my custom, I chose a word for the year. This year the word was "Purify." After last year, in which I "flirted with burnout," I wanted to purify my schedule. And I did. What I didn't realize was that God would also work to purify my beliefs, challenging me to confront and remove those lies of perfectionism I was still clinging to (see point #2). Believe me, that purification did not happen without intense times of prayer and many, many tears.

But anyway, back to the schedule. I've simplified my own schedule and commitments, along with our school schedule. I'm combining subjects, chucking some altogether, and giving ourselves much more manageable weekly assignments. We have more time to rest, relax, renew, and reconnect. And to ensure that this happens, I'm learning better how to unplug from the internet.

7. I'm remembering the importance of pre-teaching and review.
Why I neglected this before, I'll never know. One of my professors in college used the entire first 15 minutes of a 75 minute class to review the last class. Why didn't I catch on to his tactic? We humans, we forget so easily. Minds need to be prepared to remember, to function, and to learn. I don't need to get so frustrated by forgetfulness. I should *expect* forgetfulness. Why else would God tell us so often in His word to Remember?

Forgetfulness is in me, and I seem to be able to live with myself just fine. It makes me think I can learn to live with my children's forgetfulness, too. I can work to reinforce their memory through review. Not rushed, exasperated review, but easy-going, happy review. I forget. You forget. Our children forget. It's part of our nature, so take a deep breath and remember it will be OK.

I now allow more time for new concepts to sink in before I get frustrated with a child. Of course they don't know understand the concept yet. It's a tricky concept. And of course they can't perform those operations yet. They can't do it with ease yet; they haven't been doing it for decades like I have. They're not robots. They can't look at or hear a concept once and understand it. Most people can't. Rather, we must be exposed to it in different ways and at different times, preferably with a calm and unworried teacher. It's my job to be that kind of teacher.

I give more encouragement over progress than I used to. I used to desire perfection and quick mastery and treat anything less as unsatisfactory. Now I see the mental effort and praise it. Now I see the improvement and point it out. I'm also more attentive to their signs of distress, and I don't always push through. Tears, anxiety, hunger, fatigue, it's more at the front than at the back.

[BONUS TIP: I do more emotion coaching too. If someone had a poor night's sleep, or the power is out, or it's hot, or the work is just plain hard, I might say, "I know we feel like being cranky today. I feel like being cranky today. But let's try not to." I might repeat an old camp director's saying: "Make it a good day." I might tell them to switch subjects or get a snack or take a shower or do something creative or active for a while.]

8. And finally, I've started sharing and confessing in real life community.

I see how other people deal with their issues, and they see how I deal with mine. I know what other people's struggles are, and they know mine. And we don't judge each other. In fact we are here to remind each other of all these things that I've talked about so far.

Looking back, I think partaking of closer-knit community probably predates these other changes. Being with other women who are on the same journey (cross-cultural living, ministry life, *and* homeschooling) has been the impetus I needed to make other changes in my life and in my outlook. I can't speak highly enough about this. Parenting and homeschooling should be community efforts. We don't need to fly solo.

I am by no means done learning how to be a better mother. And I will never, ever be perfect. I've called these 8 points "practices" precisely because I am not done learning how to walk in these ways. They are most certainly directional changes for me, paths I must choose to walk over and over again; I must keep practicing them. And I say they are "revolutionizing" my life because although the changes happened slowly over time, family life is markedly different for all of us now. It feels like a revolution, especially when I slip back into old habits and immediately know they are not how I want to live, because I've tasted the fruit of a different tree and felt the light of a different sun.

YOU DON'T HAVE TO HOMESCHOOL PRESCHOOL

The first thing I always tell parents is that you don't have to homeschool preschool. I'm not the only one who thinks this. In fact, I don't know any homeschool moms of more than one child who do homeschool preschool. After you "do preschool" with a four-year-old child and then the next year "do kindergarten" with that same child and realize that kindergarten was just a repeat of preschool, most moms decide to ditch official preschool lessons altogether. That goes especially if you have other children in the home, either older children who actually need lessons, or babies and younger children who need a lot of hands-on care.

Here is what you actually need for the preschool years: a home full of life and love. And books. Lots and lots of books. Kids learn so naturally at this stage, and they're interested in so many things, that there's no need to do anything formal. Today I will share my favorite resources for educational theory and practice. I'll share my favorite books to read aloud with young children. I'll also include a list of sturdy educational toys that are a good foundation for a home schooling family to own, along with the very first curriculum you might want to buy.

EDUCATIONAL THEORY AND GUIDES

Cathy Duffy's 102 Top Picks for Homeschool Curriculum. This book guides you through teaching and learning styles. It's like a self-paced workshop to get you started on your journey.

Teaching from Rest by Sarah MacKenzie. This book is small but worth several re-reads. I also highly recommend her Read-Aloud Revival Podcast which is one of my favorite home school podcasts.

As your children grow, I have many more recommended books and podcasts. But these are the ones to start with.

TOYS AND GAMES TO INVEST IN

A soft globe that can't be pierced by toddler teeth. Only has the most basic details but helpful in the early years. We actually still use ours.

Peg boards. Kids can't get enough of these things, and even as an adult I love playing with peg boards.

Wedgits starter kit. Wedgits never get old.

Pattern Blocks. Kids love these.

Wooden Blocks. Lots of open-ended play opportunities here.

Catch the Match game.

Cuisenaire Rods. I'm big on manipulatives, can you tell?!

Until recently, my kids still played with all these toys. They are great for imaginative, open-ended play, either alone or while being read to.

It's also important to have lots of paper, crayons, colored pencils, and paints lying around, along with glue, tape, and scissors.

BOOKS TO READ ALOUD

In the beginning you just want to play with your kids and read aloud to them. If you have access to a library — great! If you live overseas without good library access, you may have to purchase some of these titles and transport them back in a suitcase. Get used to it — you'll be doing that a lot once you start homeschooling the elementary years.

Beatrix Potter's stories — all of them. A wonderful way to introduce your children to advanced language while they enjoy the lush illustrations. As an adult I adore Potter's stories. It's better to get them as individual books, but if you can't, a treasury will work (I usually don't recommend treasuries because of their bulk).

Mike Mulligan and More by Virginia Burton — we all love these stories, and though it's a treasury, it's not bulky.

Make Way for McCloskey. Another non-bulky treasury with the funny stories and beautiful pictures of Robert McCloskey.

Reading Mother Goose rhymes to your young kids is also great for them — it introduces them to poetry, is enjoyable, and gives them some cultural literacy.

Reading your kids Fairy Tales is also part of their cultural upbringing. *A First Book of Fairy Tales* and Hans Christian Andersen's *Fairy Tales* are good to begin with.

Anything by Arnold Lobel, especially the *Frog and Toad* books, *Owl at Home*, and *Mouse Tales*. These transition nicely from read alouds to early readers.

I'm not a huge Dr. Seuss fan, but we really like *Horton Hatches the Egg*, *Horton Hears a Who*, and *Sneetches on Beaches*.

A read aloud book from Usborne that's a lot of fun is *Farmyard Tales*. It's a treasury that's not too bulky, and the stories are fun for reading aloud and then later reading alone.

Roxaboxen by Alice McLerran. A beautiful story about imagination and community.

Corduroy and *Dandelion*, both by Don Freeman and both about home and belonging.

The Story of Ferdinand by Munro Leaf. A deceptively small story about nature, introversion, and kind mothers.

The Little Brute Family by Russell Hoban. More grown-up wisdom for the little kids (or is it little kid wisdom for the grown ups?).

Really little kids love Eric Carle books. We don't have very many of them anymore, but they're pretty much all good.

For preschool Bible times, I love *The New Bible in Pictures for Little Eyes* by Kenneth Taylor. Much more comprehensive than most children's Bibles while including a picture for each story.

When your kids are a little bit older, they will enjoy these non-picture books:

Grandma's Attic series by Arleta Richardson– fun stories that aren't too moralizing. Better than Laura Ingalls Wilder and better than *Caddie Woodlawn*.

My Father's Dragon by Ruth Stiles Gannett. Fun and easy. There are two more by that author: *The Dragons of Blueland* and *Elmer and the Dragon*.

Charlotte's Web by E.B. White. A classic.

Also popular are *Stuart Little* by E.B. White and *The Cricket in Times Square* by George Selden.

Mr. Popper's Penguins by Richard Atwater is lots of fun.

The Mouse and the Motorcycle by Beverly Cleary is also lots of fun. There are two others in the series: *Runaway Ralph* and *Ralph S. Mouse*.

Kids love Gertrude Chandler Warner's *Box Car* books. They make great read alouds and then middle grade readers.

Another popular one with older readers is *My Side of the Mountain* by Jean Craighead George.

Of course we can't neglect C.S. Lewis's *Chronicles of Narnia*. You want them as separate books.

All these stories are just as enjoyable by parents and kids, which is what you want in a home library. To buy these books all at once would be a lot of money; but I didn't buy them all at once. I bought them slowly over time. The idea here is to give your children a taste for good literature so that they aren't satisfied with lesser quality stuff.

But you do want to make sure the books you buy are books your family will love — all families are different. If you have access to a public library, you'll be able to more easily and more cheaply get a feel for which books fit your family. You can get a ton of great book ideas from Gladys Hunt's *Honey for a Child's Heart* (or access the FREE book list at the Read Aloud Revival website).

When you invest money in good books and games and toys, you'll want a special place for them, and you'll want to teach your kids how to take good care of these items so they don't get lost (or in the case of books, damaged). I like to keep books off the floor, mostly because of the constant risk of flooding in Cambodia.

That's about it. In the beginning all you need are some of those building block sets, Play-doh (homemade or store-bought; good for open-ended play), the basic art supplies I mentioned earlier, and some good books to read. Take them to the park (if you have public parks — we don't) and let them play outside. Give them basic chores to do like setting the table and putting their laundry in the bin and picking up their toys. It really doesn't have to be complicated in the early years. They're just learning what it means to live in a family.

BEGINNING CURRICULUM (FOR LATER)

As they begin reading and writing around age 5, you'll want a good math program, a good reading program, and a good writing program. Focus on that for a year or two, then slowly add more "curriculum." When your kids get older, Usborne and DK Eyewitness do have a lot of good science and history spines (spines are resource books that aren't too "textbook-y").

I use Singapore Math in the early years, but Math U See is getting consistently good reviews for being kid- and parent-friendly.

For teaching reading, I like *The Reading Lesson* because it's got big print, and you can write and color in it. I've also heard very good things about All About Reading.

I also like the Bob Books Set 1 & Set 2 and the Sonlight Kindergarten and Grade 1 readers. Young children get a lot of satisfaction from reading an entire book, and each individual book is not too much work at once — you do not want to overtax the child's mind.

Pretty much everybody I know uses *Handwriting without Tears* for handwriting. I think you can also buy the books on Amazon.

A good regular atlas and a good Bible atlas are important resources to have. The *Student Bible Atlas* is excellent. Nearly any atlas by National Geographic is a good one. I've got the *World Atlas for Young Explorers*. But there's probably a newer, more updated one now.

~~~~~~~~~~~~~~~~

Well, that's the end of my "You don't have to homeschool preschool" lecture. I hope this has been helpful to you. Feel free to contact me privately if you want more information or to talk about this more in depth.

UNREALISTIC EXPECTATIONS (HOME SCHOOL BURNOUT PART 1)

August, 2015

I wanted to quit homeschooling this year. I had two separate crises in fact. I got to a place where I didn't know what was wrong; I only knew something wasn't working. I felt overwhelmed all the time. I couldn't figure out how to fit the responsibilities of motherhood, homeschooling, and writing into my life. I kept thinking that one of those three things had to go. It obviously couldn't be motherhood (duh!), so which of the other two was it going to be?

I got to the end of most school days and didn't want any more kid-interaction. I just wanted to quit and go hide somewhere. I wasn't playing games with my kids anymore, I wasn't reading aloud to them, I wasn't enjoying them. I felt guilty about my lack of interaction. I complained to my husband that homeschooling was stealing my motherhood. This wasn't what all the home school speakers and writers promised would happen if I chose to home school. Everything was supposed to be peaches and cream! Rainbows and butterflies! Pony rides in May sunshine!

A friend (and fellow home school mom) said I sounded like I was in burnout. My husband kept asking me if I wanted to put the kids in school. I kept hesitating. We were finally able to sit down to talk about homeschooling in January. I'm the kind of person who feels overwhelmed and doesn't even know where to *begin* problem-solving. I need someone to talk it out with me and guide me through it.

So we talked. We talked about what homeschooling gives our family. Things like:
1.   We can take our vacations and home assignments whenever, and sick days are easy to make up.

2.   We have long leisurely family breakfasts where we sit and talk together.

3.   We don't have to get up at the crack of dawn to have said family breakfast.

4.   As long as the environment is quiet and peaceful, I do actually enjoy teaching, especially   subjects like math and science.

We also talked about what made homeschooling so stressful for me. I had to think for a while to come up with answers that didn't include the word "everything":

1. **I was extremely far behind on read-alouds and it was majorly stressing me out.** Our Sonlight curriculum chooses historical fiction novels that correspond to our history lessons, and Mom is supposed to read them aloud during the school day. I was really uptight about these read-alouds. I feared my children would not receive a thorough education if they did not hear me read all this historical fiction to them. But I couldn't find consistent time to read the books. The daily readings were rather long. That meant I would get really behind if I missed even one day, and by that time I had missed a *lot* of days. **I felt perpetually behind and would not allow myself to read something for fun if I hadn't finished the "assigned" book. This meant we never read anything for fun.** The Sonlight read-alouds are *supposed* to be fun, but to me they still felt like school, and I wasn't having any fun. On top of that, I missed reading to my kids. When they were younger and had less schoolwork to do, I was able to read to them for hours each day. All the Sonlight books, plus extras from the library. With the loss of read-alouds, I felt like my bonding time with my kids had been snatched away.
2. I worried over what I would do if I ever had trouble teaching a particular subject to a particular child.
3. There was also the fact that four children in one house can get rather loud rather quickly. Chaos due to age gaps is what home school moms have to deal with if they happen to have more than one child. How to keep your young ones quietly entertained while older ones work? That is the age-old

question for home school moms, and its answer had been eluding me.

4. Additionally, I had been freaking out for years about how to teach four different levels at the same time. Even when I was only teaching 2 levels, I worried about adding the 3rd and 4th. I dragged this fear around with me each year. I carried it through each day I didn't quite finish everything I intended to finish. I was so afraid of what the future would hold. (Worry is a common theme with me, have you noticed?)

At this point my husband noted something important: Sending the kids to school wouldn't cure all my parenting woes. School wasn't some magic elixir. I might not have the burden of teaching them, true, but I'd have to get up early each morning to get them ready to leave. I'd have to pack lunches each day and check homework and organize transportation to and from school. We wouldn't have our peaceful, unrushed mornings, and I knew I would miss that family time. **Sending my kids to school, just like schooling them at home, was going to have both pros and cons.**

So we talked about targeted solutions for specific problems. Most of these solutions came in the form of *permission*. Permission not to read the assigned historical fiction. Permission to read what I want to read to them. Permission to get tutors or outside help if I ever felt the need.

Permission. Was it really that simple?? All I know is that releasing some of those expectations lifted a huge weight off my shoulders. Astonishing how such a simple statement ("I don't have to read the Sonlight read-alouds") could so unburden me. Oh I knew in theory that you can't do every Sonlight assignment. The company says that. Experienced Sonlight moms say that. But I had never internalized it. I had never applied it to my own classroom. Now I had the chance.

Next on the to-do list was searching for a good time to actually read together. As I mentioned, even though I wanted to read, I was having difficulty finding the space in our days. When I stopped pressuring myself to read Sonlight's books, when the read-aloud timeline was lifted, I found I *could* squeeze reading into our day.

I started reading aloud during lunchtime. Now, I eat quickly and read while everyone else eats. When we finish eating, I clean up, and we move to the living room where we keep reading. With this approach I'm able to read about 45 minutes each day, and **we all love reading together again.**

I didn't find a solution for my fears about teaching four levels at once. I just sort of put the worry off until tomorrow. But hey, that's Biblical, right? "Therefore do not worry about tomorrow, for tomorrow will worry about itself. Each day has enough trouble of its own." Relinquishing the expectation to read every single Sonlight read aloud was enough for now. I could deal with the other stuff later.

"MOM FAIL" (HOME SCHOOL BURNOUT PART 2)

August, 2015

Our January discussion helped a lot, but then I just charged ahead into spring and overcommitted myself to the blogging world. It feels awkward to admit that, but it's true. I severely underestimated my time and energy commitments — though in my defense, I didn't realize I was overcommitting myself at the time.

I had wanted to write about the "Parsonage Heresies" (see The Little Word That Frees Us) for about a year, and in January I finally decided to do it on A Life Overseas. I didn't realize that series was going to be such an emotional, intellectual, and time drain. Committing myself to a specific subject and needing to write an in-depth post about it every month really wore me out. Don't get me wrong, I am so glad I wrote this series! It was just draining.

I also committed to write two Velvet Ashes posts for the spring. These weren't ordinary posts though. They were related to the heavy themes in the book *Expectations and Burnout* and were also an emotional and time drain. Again, I'm so glad I wrote these! Especially Jesus Loves Me This I Sometimes Know (on Velvet Ashes) — that story simply burned in my heart to be told.

By the time I got to early May, however, I was exhausted. I had spent myself in writing. In order to meet all the deadlines, I had directed attention away from my children. **Somewhere in the process of writing and reaching out to the women who connected with my stories, I had inadvertently turned my heart away from my children, and now I didn't particularly feel like turning back.** Noise was still a stressor during school days, and I had a hard time fitting everyone's lessons around my grueling blogging schedule, so I felt really behind again. I know six articles in four months doesn't seem like it warrants the description "grueling," but these posts took a lot from me.

I was poured out and empty. I took time off from blogging at other sites and condensed a couple weeks of school into one week in order to finish the school year a bit earlier. I thought I was going to lose my mind, and I needed a break. I was so tired. I told my husband I wanted to go away for a year; he told me that was an unreasonable solution. I knew he was right. I also knew I needed some way to refresh and refuel, and I didn't know how long would be enough.

So when the first Monday of summer break came around, I took a break from parenting — almost literally. I let myself be a "bad" mom: I locked myself in my bedroom and let my children watch movies. All.day.long. I didn't talk to them, I didn't read to them, I didn't play with them. It was a total "mom fail."

I knew I only had four weeks of summer break because of our upcoming stateside service, and I wanted squeeze every last second out of it. I watched movies. I played Freecell. I read books. I wasted time on Facebook. I didn't blog. I wasn't productive. I was in a very fragile state and needed to be alone.

By the end of that first week I discovered, to my surprise, that perhaps I didn't need an *entire* year away. Perhaps these few weeks would be enough of a break. Already I felt like coming out of my bedroom and interacting with my family again. Not all the time, mind you, just some of the time. I still hung out in my bedroom a lot.

During the third week God did something in my heart. It began with a prayer session at church where I started asking the question, "Why don't I want to give my children my time?" That week as I started seeking answers to that question, another home school mom asked how she could pray for me. I didn't share all the details, but I confided that I needed help balancing teaching and writing. (This was true, but rather general.)

It felt good to know someone was praying about this issue for me, because up to that point I hadn't done much of that. Her prayers must have been working because the very next day I tuned in to a Sonlight webinar, and it reminded me why I love teaching my children and why I decided to do it in the first place. Those three events were pivotal in renewing my desire to home school.

So as summer drew to a close, I started recovering my heart for homeschooling. I started recovering my heart for my children. I started reorienting my heart toward my children, turning *toward* them instead of away. And by the time school started four weeks ago, I was ready to teach again. I was ready to spend time together again. I was ready to love again.

I still had to figure out the practicalities of fitting four students' lessons into each day. (Eek! My long-time fears actually started materializing this school year!) I still had to figure out how to get all my writing and editing jobs done on time. But God had addressed my heart problem. He had given me the rest and recuperation I needed. He had supernaturally given me the ability to look at my summer "mom fails" not as a failure but as a *necessity*. In short, He had allowed my non-productive summer to be really productive.

THE MEAN MOMMY (HOME SCHOOL BURNOUT PART 3)

August, 2015

There's more to the story than Part 1: Unrealistic Expectations and Part 2: Mom Fail. Much more went on in my heart the last couple weeks of summer break, and I really wrestled with whether to share what I'm about to share. I'm fiercely protective of my children's privacy, and I don't share much about them online (more on why I've chosen to do that in a couple weeks at Velvet Ashes).

I was afraid that talking about my homeschooling struggles might reveal that *gasp! I've ever had parenting issues at all (as though both my children and I are perfect)*. While I never want to share my children's stories or betray their confidences, this story wasn't actually about them. It was about me and my own sin, and that's something I do feel (timidly) comfortable sharing. **I also felt it would be disingenuous to leave the story at "God turned my heart towards my children that week and POOF! Everything was fixed." It wasn't that simple or straightforward.**

God softened my heart that third week of summer, it's true. But something else happened after that: I listened to a free, one-time webinar called "Teaching Ramona Quimby: Homeschooling Your Intense Child." I signed up for this webinar because, um, FREE. (I also listened to a free one about teaching math conceptually, but that doesn't have much to do with this part of the story.)

The speaker listed some of the characteristics of what she calls the "intense child." As I listened I recognized *myself* in her description. *I* was an intense child, all grown up. **I have big internal reactions to stuff, I'm sensitive to external stimuli, I don't like my routine altered, I want to blame other people for my upsets, and I don't always know what to do with my emotions.**

I began to see that I was aggravating the homeschool stress through my reactions and attitudes. Busted! God was convicting me big time. You mean this all came back to me? You mean I'm the problem

80

here? I didn't want to admit that. I would rather blame my issues on something *outside* me. I really couldn't though.

I started having some conversations with my husband about this stuff, and we talked more in-depth about "boundaries." He'd been telling me for a while that I didn't have good boundaries, though at the time I'd been so overwhelmed I didn't really know what he meant or how to implement his advice. As I became convicted that my own behavior was causing my frustrations, I could now look inside and see he was right.

Here is what I found inside myself: a deep fear of being a Mean Mommy. There's a voice in my head that tells me I have to be available to my children at all hours. I can never tell them no (see: I'm Not Supposed to Have Needs). So I would let little people climb on me all the time. I couldn't give myself permission to take a break or to tell them no. In my mind that would be withholding love, and I wasn't supposed to do that.

I didn't want to be mean. I didn't want to reject anybody. But when my patience had worn thin and I was tired of being climbed on, I did reject. I snapped and spoke unkindly, or I went away and hid. Or both. Result: **I was becoming the Mean Mommy I was trying so hard to avoid.** Ouch! That realization hurt.

So I started seeing myself as culpable. I needed to take responsibility for my behavior and my reactions. I needed to institute some better boundaries, and I needed to do it calmly. I found that when I did, peace returned to my home. I fell in love with my children again. I was able to see and care for their little hearts again. I even *delighted* in them again.
The Mommy I was meant to be was coming back from the grave.

7 THOUGHTS FOR GRADUATING TCKs

Dear Graduating Senior,

This spring I hugged you. I cried with you. I said goodbye to you.
And then I looked into the faces of your parents as they said goodbye
too. How can I express the depth of my love for you and your
parents? I don't know. All I know is that if we were sitting down to
coffee again, these are the things I'd want to tell you.
They're the things I've mostly stumbled across on my journey as an
Adult Third Culture Kid, though they're by no means comprehensive
or applicable to all people. Much like every other human on the
planet, I've had to sort through my childhood as an adult, and these
are the things that have helped me along the way. I hope they help
you too.

1. IT'S OK (AND NORMAL) TO HAVE DELAYED ISSUES

When you were young, home was where mom and dad were (or
perhaps where grandma and grandpa were), and most likely, you were
almost always with one of those people or in one of those places. But
TCK angst is something that tends to catch up to people later in life.
That's the way it was for me, anyway.

Issues of home, belonging, and identity are all higher level, more
complex topics. And now that you're launching out on your own,
your old idea of "home" probably won't be as accessible. The Third
Culture world of your childhood will be out of reach, and these issues
might come crashing down on you. **All of this is OK.**

Maybe you felt settled in life before, but feel unsettled now. Maybe
you thought life was good or even great before, but feel lost now.
Maybe you were part of a happy, healthy family as a child and now
find yourself dealing with some thorny emotional issues as a young
adult. Don't worry; it doesn't mean anything is wrong with you.

Or perhaps you've already experienced a lot of transition and upheaval in your life, and you've already had to grapple with issues of belonging, identity, and home. That's ok too. You'll probably still find that TCK issues pop up in your life over the next several years, often when you're not expecting them. **This is normal. It's part of the process of growing up.** I just don't want you to be surprised by it.

2. SYSTEMS ARE A HELPFUL LENS

Growing up as a military kid, I didn't have a vocabulary for what was happening in my life. For example, why was civilian life so different and so hard for us?? Answer: because we had suddenly exited a military system (or culture) and entered a non-military one. I didn't know that back then, but I know it now, and the idea of viewing the TCK experience through the lens of a *system* has been very helpful to me.

This is one way to explain the idea: your parents made a conscious choice to enter a system (whichever system it was), but much of your TCK experience was then dictated by that system. Even graduating from high school and having to leave your childhood home — as painful as that can be — is dictated by the system you're living in. You can even be part of more than one system. There's your third culture system with other TCKs. Then there's your parents' organization's system. And there are probably more.

Being able to see my life as part of a system (or systems) with a lot of moving parts has allowed me to look at some of the TCK issues I've faced as an adult without faulting my parents. Yes, the many moves were traumatic for me (and in ways I didn't realize, feel, or fully understand until I was an adult), but I don't see that trauma as being inflicted on me by my parents. Yes, they chose the military, but it wasn't their fault when the military moved us mid-school year. It wasn't their fault when kids at my new school didn't accept me right away. Rather, it was a result of the system I was in.

The ability to have conversations without shame or blame is vital to moving forward. And the more we can understand the systems we're in, the easier it is to talk about our experiences and make connections instead of disconnections. So remember that you're living in (and have lived in) a system. Remember that accepting your TCK experience doesn't mean you have to become estranged from your family. Admitting that you struggle to find belonging or to define home or self doesn't mean you're labeling your parents as "bad." These things are results of your systems.

3. ALL PEOPLE ARE SINNERS, SO REMEMBER TO GIVE GRACE

While it's true that you don't need to blame your parents for the challenges of TCK life, it's also true that they are human beings. They're sinners, just like you and just like me. And they may have made some mistakes in life as well as in parenting. Forgive them.

There's no way around the fact that human parents do hurt their human children: all humans hurt other humans. So while you don't have to carry around some burden of thinking your parents "ruined your life" with their nomadic choices, you probably also need to forgive them for things. All children — mobile and non-mobile alike — are faced with this question.

I love my parents deeply, and they deeply love me, yet we still found it necessary to have these kinds of conversations. We avoided it for a long time, perhaps for fear of conflict or discomfort, but the healing never came until we did. **So talk to your parents. Have conversations with them**. Process through the painful stuff. Wade into the murky waters, and find healing and wholeness together. Your parents are invested in your continued health and healing, so let them be a part of it.

Your situation may be more complicated than what I've just discussed. Someone may have hurt you deeply, even abused you. In that case, you need more than simple conversations with your parents or other trusted adults. You also need to get some outside help. You need to find trustworthy, compassionate counseling. Both Lisa McKay and Kay Bruner have good insight on how to find a counselor in general and while living overseas. I pray you find someone to guide you through the healing process.

4. GET COMFORTABLE WITH PARADOX

As you pack up your boxes and your suitcases, there's one more thing I want you to pack. That thing is your ability to accept and even embrace paradox. Most likely, your life has been neither one hundred percent good, nor one hundred percent bad. The truth is, TCK or not, no one's life is one hundred percent one thing. **So resist the temptation to spin the story of your childhood in only one direction, either all good or all bad.** Don't pit the good and bad against each other in a futile effort to discover which one outweighs the other.

You don't have to minimize the bad in order to accept the good. And you don't have to minimize the good in order to accept the bad. Simply hold them both in your hands and in your heart, and <u>accept them together</u>, side by side, as the things that have shaped you into the person you are and as the things that are continuing to shape the person you are becoming.

We can't strain the bad out of the good or the good out of the bad; we can't separate them like cream from milk. They're a package deal, a paradox, the "and" of this life. So let's agree together not to outlaw the good or outlaw the bad. Let's accept all the parts of ourselves, even the parts that make us (or other people) uncomfortable.

5. GRIEVE YOUR LOSSES

About those negative experiences . . . I know this has been talked about before, but it's so important I'm going to say it again: you've got to grieve your losses. List out your losses, and then <u>mourn them</u>. Grieve the hard things that happened to you.

Maybe it was leaving your passport country to move to your host country, or moving between host countries, or within the same host country. Maybe it was losing a close friend or teacher to transition or even death. It's probably graduating and leaving your host country this summer. Regardless of the cause, there have been <u>so many goodbyes in your life</u>, and you need to acknowledge how hard they've been for you.

Grief follows us wherever we go; we can't outrun it. So spend the time now, on the front end, to grieve your TCK losses. You need to learn this skill because you'll have to use it again later. **We live in a fallen world, and bad things will keep happening to you, whether you're living cross-culturally or not.** That means the need to process grief is ever-present, regardless of who you are or where you live.

Learning to grieve well now will help you for the rest of your life. And you might have to grieve some of your losses more than once. **You may feel old losses cycling back around again, and you'll have to stop and re-grieve them. That's ok.** Be gentle with yourself and grieve them again.

6. GET SOME OUTSIDE HELP: TCK COUNSELORS AND MENTORS

I personally used to think something was wrong with *me*. Why did I have all these problems fitting in? Why did I feel so rejected all the time? I thought the problem was me. Then — and this only happened a couple of years ago with a counselor who specializes in TCKs — I began to see that the trouble I had fitting in was a consequence of something that happened *to* me.

It wasn't me that was the problem; it was all those moves and having to fit in someplace new over and over and over again. But learning how to fit in takes time, and there's always a period of uncertainty before friends are made and acceptance is granted. I cannot even explain how much that realization helped me. I felt less like a broken object and more like a person who'd had experiences that shaped me but who wasn't inherently and eternally screwed up. I had previously faced a lot of insecurity and social anxiety in my life, but when I started seeing their roots in my nomadic childhood and addressing them that way, the fear and insecurity stopped trailing me so doggone much.

Likewise, you may need a counselor who is familiar with the TCK world. In fact, in her book Belonging Everywhere and Nowhere:

Insights into Counseling the Globally Mobile, author and counselor Lois Bushong tells us that a counselor who is not familiar with TCK issues may not know how to treat an adult TCK struggling with depression. In actuality, he or she is probably dealing with unresolved TCK grief, a completely normal response to a globally mobile childhood. (Incidentally Lois is also responsible for my understanding of systems.) **So if you are in any way "stuck" in your emotional, mental, or spiritual life, consider finding a counselor who understands TCK life.**

Counseling has been massively helpful in my life, both for TCK-related issues and non-TCK-related issues, and I highly recommend counseling to all people who are breathing. But sometimes you just need someone to talk to, someone who will listen to you and empathize with you and even pray for you. Just talking to an older, wiser adult TCK whom you trust can be very helpful in sorting through your thoughts and feelings. In fact, I've done that a lot with Marilyn Gardner, fellow writer and editor on this blog. **So if you do nothing else, find a fellow TCK friend to talk to.**

7. YOU SHOULD PROBABLY EXPECT SOME FLARE-UPS

I can give you all the advice in the world — advice you might even follow — but you might still turn around one day and be taken by surprise at the intensity of your feelings of loss and isolation and lack of home and belonging. When this happens to me, whether it's triggered by the yearly May & June goodbyes or by feeling the sting of some rejection, my husband usually asks me, **"Is your TCK acting up again?"**

Yes, I tell him. The answer is almost always yes. Yes that my TCK is acting up again. Yes that events from my childhood creep into my adulthood. Yes that from time to time issues I thought were settled and resolved feel suddenly unsettled and unresolved.

But simply naming it can take the edge off the pain. Then I can go back to the truths I've learned about myself and about God. And you can do that too. When you find your TCK acting up again, name it. Grieve what you need to grieve, and then remind yourself of the truths you've learned over the years. Be kind to yourself when this happens, and remember to give yourself some time to recover.

~~~~~~~~~~~~~~~~~~~~~~~

Even though there was pain, I don't regret my TCK experience. For me every experience (in the end) brought me closer to Christ. Though at times it might have seemed a wandering path, every wound was a road leading straight back to God. The relationship I have <u>with God</u> primarily because of painful TCK "issues" is something I wouldn't give up for anything.

So take heart. If you let them, the questions of home, belonging, and identity that your TCK childhood has asked you to answer can take you deeper into the heart of God than ever before. If you'll take the time to look for Him, you'll find Jesus on the other side of every question you have. Only Jesus can help you live an unhindered life. His is the face of love, and He is the answer to every question you'll ever ask. So go with Him: **there is redemption on this road.**

ON YOUR HIGH SCHOOL GRADUATION: A LETTER TO MY THIRD CULTURE KIDS

I've been watching parents in the international community say goodbye to their graduating seniors for a while now. I've been watching the seniors themselves say goodbye to their friends – fellow third culture kids like themselves.

Watching these parental goodbyes feels like a knife in my chest. I have to stop myself from thinking about it just so I can breathe again. Because I know that will be me, someday, saying goodbye to *you*.

"**Goodbye.**" We get a lot of practice saying it. We've said goodbye to short-term workers. They never planned to stay, but we welcomed them into our lives anyway. We've said goodbye to others — longer term workers whose time in this country, for a variety of reasons, has also come to a close.

And then, every year, I watch the graduating high school seniors. The ones who leave their families behind and travel to their passport country for their university years —and beyond.

As I write this, all four of you are more than eight years away from entering your college years. Still, someday I will say goodbye to each of you in turn. My oldest son first, then a couple years later, my youngest son. A couple years after that, I will be saying goodbye to my oldest daughter. The next goodbye will be my last. My youngest daughter will leave too.

I must say goodbye to you like this, no matter where in the world I live. And when you do leave, there are things I want to tell you. Things like. . .

You are my child. You are now an adult, and I'm proud of who you are, but you will always be part of my family. **Our home can always be your home.** No matter where we live, we will always welcome you into it.

89

We have endeavored to give you as stable a home life as possible in the ever-shifting international community in which we live. **I am sorry** for the consistent, repeated, prolonged, never-ending goodbyes you have endured. **So say goodbye well.** For many of your high school friends, the goodbye may be forever. You might return to Cambodia; you might not. And your friends may not. Even if they do, it most likely wouldn't be at the same time as you. So honor your friends with good goodbyes.

Keep in touch with your TCK friends if you can. After my military upbringing I finally found a small group of friends in high school. They were Christians. They buoyed my life and my faith at the time, and I regret not keeping in touch with them. Even with Facebook, I've only been able to find a couple of them, and I wish I could find more. So stay in touch. You won't regret it. This journey has already separated you from many friends, so strive to keep the ones that still remain.

There won't be any weekend trips home for you, as I had. You'll live more than just a few hours away. So you'll have to say goodbye to this place, not just the people. Again, make sure you say goodbye well. **Write these places, and their memories, on your heart forever.**

I was lonely and depressed my first year at college. My roommate was never around, and my hourly venture to the water fountain was the most exciting thing I did while I studied. Don't do that; don't be like me. I sequestered myself in my room. More time at a park probably would have lifted my low spirits, so **for goodness sakes, go to a park every once in a while.**

I did find friends in a campus ministry. **So whatever you do, find a good campus ministry.** A community of your peers following hard after God. Form deep friendships there, deep enough to last your whole life long. My campus ministry friends still inspire me to love Jesus more, and to serve Him in both the little things and the big things.

Find a good church. A church that loves, a church that lives and breathes and teaches both Grace and Truth. Churches are flawed because the people are flawed. But **if the Grace is there, it will cover over the flaws.** Hopefully these people will feed you and lend you their laundry rooms, and maybe even sometimes, when you really need it, their cars. They will be there to catch you when you fall to loneliness and depression and temptation. They will be people with whom you can worship every Sunday. Your studying will exhaust you, and **you won't feel like getting up on Sunday mornings, but if you show up, you will find God there.**

Try to live your life in real time, with real people. **Don't waste your time getting drunk, playing video games, or looking at trashy pictures on the internet. That stuff doesn't satisfy.** But even if you do turn to those things, your Papa and I will always welcome you with open arms. We are always your family. Our hearts are open, our home is open. Possibly more importantly right now, though, is that **our inboxes are always open.**

And whatever happens, you *must* know that your Heavenly Father will always welcome you Home. He is always there for you. He will forgive anything. **And should you ever stray from Him, don't stay away forever out of fear that He doesn't want you.** He wants you. Believe it.

All my love,
Mom

The Theologian/Christian Woman/Trying my best Hat

I grew up hearing sermons about the "goodness and severity of God" and about God not hearing the prayer of the sinner. Girls Bible study times were filled with questions like, "If women are to remain silent in church, is it a sin to whisper in church to ask someone the song number if I didn't hear it announced?" and "How long should my shorts be?" So by the time I entered ministry at the age of 19, no one had to tell me I needed to be perfect; I already knew I needed to be perfect. And not only did I know I needed to be perfect, I knew everyone else needed to be perfect as well.

At the same time, I knew everyone wasn't perfect. As a teenager, I knew my church friends were being physically and sexually abused at home, but no one would ever dare talk about that at church, where their dads were leaders. This taught me that the families around me weren't perfect; it also taught me that they needed to appear that way. Furthermore, it taught me that the rest of us needed to treat them as though they were perfect. **The appearance of perfection mattered more than actual righteousness.**

Those are my stories; your stories will be different. Yet our collective stories may have taught us something dark and devious: that ministry and missionary families are (or should be) holier than everyone else. Our stories may have taught us that in order to serve God, we need to be super human. At the very least, our stories may have taught us that we need to project an image of perfection. Sometimes we extend this expectation to others and become judgmental of their non-perfection; other times we require it only of ourselves.

Of course, none of us is perfect. We all know this very well, because we all wrestle with our own sin natures. So we can become discouraged when we fail to meet our self-imposed (or church-imposed) "shoulds" over, and over, and over again. The pressures placed on missionaries, ministers, and their wives and children are often unattainable and put them at risk for depression. **The painful** irony here is that since they're "supposed" to be perfect and not have any "major" problems, there's shame both in the depression (or other mental health issues) and its appropriate treatment.

To illustrate this, Sanford once took an informal survey at a PK conference, asking for a show of hands of people who had been diagnosed with depression, placed on anti-depressant medicine, or hospitalized for depression. **80% of attendants raised their hands**, at which point a woman in the back piped up with "But we're not allowed to be!"

James says in his letter that "We all stumble in many ways," and John's first letter tells us, "If we claim we have no sin, we are only fooling ourselves and not living in the truth." So the truth is, we can't be perfect, and we don't have to be. Yes, some of us are better than others at appearing perfect, but nobody actually is perfect. We sin, we mess up, we fail. Regularly. I repeat: we don't have to be perfect. We don't even have to give the impression.

Now this is much easier to say than it is to live. All those things I'd learned in church? Well, they had impacted my conception of God and who I was in relation to Him. I hadn't realized it before, but **I had zero theology of Grace.** I thought I needed to prove my worth and earn my salvation. It was only about eight years ago that I began deconstructing these harmful beliefs. For about four months that year, I met with a counselor once a week. I spent lots of time in prayer with my Bible study group, and I read lots of Paul: Ephesians, Galatians, Romans. (I'm unabashed about my love for Paul.) Over and over and over again I listened and cried and danced to Chris Tomlin's cover of Matt Maher's song "Your Grace Is Enough." These things transformed my thinking about sin and grace.

That year was a turning point in my walk with God and my understanding of Grace. I relinquished the old ways of thinking — though I confess they still creep back to haunt me from time to time. In those times, I have to return to God and ask Him to renew my mind yet again. (And yes, when I forget Grace, I still sometimes beat myself up by thinking, "I should understand this better by now!")

Our attempts to be perfect cripple our experience of Christ. His perfection, and His perfection alone, undergirds the entire Gospel. And the Gospel is completely counter-cultural, in every culture. This is why we sometimes struggle to accept it: it seems quite literally too good to be true. Except that it is true! Grace, full and free, releases us from the requirements we feel from church members and supporters (and ourselves) to meet some impossible standard of perfection that Jesus already met. **In Christ Alone, our hope is found.**

Grace isn't necessarily easy medicine to swallow for us perfectionists. I would often cry my eyes out in a counseling session and then be so exhausted I could sleep for the rest of the day. A single blog post cannot easily dismantle our beliefs surrounding God's approval and our efforts. Unraveling our thinking is, frustratingly, not an overnight process. I do believe, however, that it's a process He is faithful to fulfill.

"I'm damned if I do and damned if I don't"

This phrase reflects the Either/Or mindset that has plagued me for so much of my life. It's this kind of black-and-white thinking that has gotten me into so much inner turmoil: If I make one mistake, then I must be a total failure. And depression ensues. The "damned if I do and damned if I don't" attitude also gives way to futility: If I can't do something perfectly, then I won't do it at all. This goes for "spiritual" things like Bible reading and also seemingly less spiritual things like interpersonal conflict and offering apologies.

The tragedy of Either/Or thinking is that it doesn't acknowledge paradox or complexity. It doesn't acknowledge that sanctification is a process. It doesn't acknowledge that we are not fully regenerate yet and that no, we are not there yet. These are truths my beloved Apostle Paul acknowledged. (Romans 7 and Philippians 3, anyone?)

Brennan Manning said, "When I get honest, I admit that I am a bundle of paradoxes. I believe and I doubt, I hope and I get discouraged, I love and I hate, I feel bad about feeling good, I feel guilty about not feeling guilty. I am trusting and suspicious. I am honest and I still play games. To live by grace means to acknowledge my whole life's story, the light side and the dark." According to Manning, living by grace means embracing all the <u>ANDS</u> of our lives. (Don't you just love Brennan Manning??)

When AND isn't a part of our collective vocabulary, we tend to believe we are judged as either 100% good or 100% bad, with no middle ground. We feel stuck. **We know everything is not all right, both in our own personal lives and in our families' lives, but since image is more important than reality (as we discussed earlier), we don't feel the freedom to tell the whole truth.** In a way, this is a consequence of believing we have to be perfect — and if we're not, we just better keep our mouths shut about it.

I still don't know why I didn't feel free to tell anybody about my friends being abused. I wasn't being abused at home; so why should I have been scared to tell anyone about my friends, whom I loved? Perhaps I had picked up on the idea that the Church is "supposed" to keep silent about these things. Just let the leaders lead; the abuse they perpetrate against their children at home has nothing to do with their reasonable service at church. Just let the teachers teach; the pain they inflict on their children at home has nothing to do with their reasonable service at church. The unspoken rule becomes: Keep these things secret. Don't ever tell the truth. Speak up, and you'll be punished. Speak out, and you'll be judged as rebellious.

It's hard to keep the ugly truth bottled up all the time, and it tends to leak out in one way or another. One way it leaks out is by escaping into another world. In particular, Sanford says people use food (either binging, binging and purging, or restricting) and sex (mostly porn) as escapes, as some of these can be hidden, at least for a time. He says the truth also tends to slip out in sarcasm, which sometimes seems bitter and angry. However, sarcasm and escapes may not be our main problem: they may only be the mechanism we're using to tell our stories.

So what is the cure for "Damned if I do, damned if I don't"? I believe it's to allow ourselves to say AND. **It's to allow ourselves, as Brennan Manning said, to be honest and admit we are a bundle of paradoxes, and to allow each other to say it as well.** It's when we acknowledge our whole life's story, the light side and the dark side, that we can begin to live by Grace alone.

"God is disappointed with me"

The lies in this series are all somewhat related, and this last one closely follows "I have to be perfect." It represents the fear that if I'm not perfect, then God will be mad at me. That if I make a mistake (or several), He'll disapprove of me. We can spend our whole lives trying to make God happy with our behavior. Working, working, working, trying so very hard to please Him.

This one is listed last in the book because it's what Sanford calls a **"holy heresy about God."** The others lies are about myself and others, but this one goes straight to the heart of God. Sometimes when we grow up in church, we get the idea that God is just waiting for us to make a mistake so He can bring down His wrath, and punish us once and for all. We get the idea that we don't deserve His love and aren't good enough to earn His forgiveness. Not that He delights in us and sings over us, not that He loves us with an everlasting love and has saved us by His own Hand.

If that's the kind of angry, vengeful God we know, we might end up walking away from Him.

I won't even pretend to have all the answers here for how to deal with this lie. It goes really deep and takes a lot of time to shed. What I hope to do is to give you some resources that have helped me deal with this lie. I pray they can deepen your intimacy with God and strengthen your trust in His love.

Beginning to walk in the assurance of God's unconditional love for us is an intensely personal journey. We walk part of it together, in <u>safe</u> community. We must also walk some of it alone, in the secret places of our hearts. It's when I close the metaphorical door of my prayer closet and meet with God one on one that He touches me most personally and most deeply. I pray God will grant more and more of those sweet times of fellowship to all of us.

RESOURCES FOR ENCOUNTERING GOD

Brennan Manning

I mentioned Brennan Manning earlier in the post. The summer after I finished that four-month stint of counseling was my first introduction to Brennan Manning. My husband led our youth group through the *Ragamuffin Gospel, Visual Edition*. It's an abridged version of his original work, with art. It was a balm to my soul and cemented in my mind the things I'd been learning that year.

This year I've been going through the daily devotions in Manning's *Reflections for Ragamuffins*. Each day has a Scripture and a selection from his other writings. This year I've been on a journey to know God's love more, and this book has been a big part of that.

A Life Overseas writer Kay Bruner recommends *Abba's Child*. Although I haven't read it, I love Manning enough and trust Kay enough to recommend it here.

Henri Nouwen

I'd never read anything from Henri Nouwen before this Lenten season, when a friend of mine in Phnom Penh gave me a copy of *Show Me the Way*. It's a collection of excerpts from his many books, and it's profoundly affected my relationship with God. I loved Nouwen's Lent book so much that I asked my friend for more recommendations (though I haven't been able to get my hands on them yet). Again, I love Nouwen enough and trust my friend enough to include them below.

Return of the Prodigal Son

Life of the Beloved, which was her husband's favorite

Jeanne Guyon

Jeanne Guyon wrote a book called *Experiencing the Depths of Jesus* that affected author Timothy Sanford so deeply that he recommends it in his Parsonage Heresies book.

The Bible

I know I've recommended Paul's letters already, but I love Paul so much, I'll say it again. Especially Ephesians, Galatians, and Romans. Hebrews is also helpful, but then, we don't know who wrote that.

The book of First John. Also helpful is Beth Moore's explanation of the life of John and his relationship with Jesus. Moore's *Beloved Disciple* Bible study rewrote my understanding of the Apostle John.

The Psalms. I've often felt God's love through the Psalms. (And I'm betting you probably have too.)

I Corinthians 13, viewed as a letter to you, from God. We know that God is love, and I Corinthians 13 is one of our best descriptions of what love looks like practically. **I Corinthians 13 therefore gives us a glimpse into how God sees and treats us.** This is an exercise Sanford recommends that made a big impact on me when I first read it a year and a half ago. Write it out in your own handwriting, use your own name, and ask God to show you His great big heart for you.

Music

Music is a huge part of my connection with God. In particular, worship music from the International House of Prayer (IHOP) has opened up a whole new aspect of God for me: His passionate love for me and my reciprocal love for Him. IHOP music leans toward the charismatic end of the spectrum; two really gentle introductions to their music are listed below.

Unceasing, especially "Alabaster Box" on Track 5 and "I am Yours" on Track 12

JOY, especially "Every Captive Free" on Track 5 and "Marriage Wine" on Track 3. **"My dad, He's not angry. He's not disappointed with me. My dad, He's not angry. He's smiling over me"**

PAUL THE MISOGYNIST

While this tends to be a faith-walk type of blog, and not a theology blog, I'd be a fool not to admit that some of my biggest personal crises happen at the intersection of faith and theology. As this is an enormous subject, and as I am not a Bible scholar, this post is not meant to offer an authoritative stance on my part, or even to start a debate: it is simply an important part of my faith journey that I feel the need to share. I asked God to help me write something that honors Him but that expresses my struggle to understand certain parts of the New Testament, and this is the result.

I always loved the apostle Peter. It seemed to me that he said whatever he was thinking before he had time to think about it. He was impulsive, given to emotional outbursts, and faltered under fear — and I could relate. Yet Peter always returned to Jesus, and he lived Forgiven.

Paul, on the other hand, was never quite so important to me. I only started getting to know him several years ago, in a counselor's office, as I worked through the concept of grace. Week after week I sat on that couch in the counselor's office, crying, trying desperately to understand the doctrine of Grace, trying to accept the fact that God loves me completely, apart from anything I do or don't do.

It was truly some of the hardest work I've ever had to do, and it was during this period that I fell in love with Paul's letters, especially the books of Romans, Galatians, and Ephesians. His teachings rescued my relationship with God and gave me the strength to move forward in a deeper understanding of Grace and the Cross of Christ. I learned that I can do nothing good enough to earn His love, that I can do nothing bad enough to stop His love. **He simply loves and forgives on His own merit, not on mine**.

Years later, cracks would appear in my relationship with Paul's writings. Texts like Colossians 3, I Corinthians 11 and 14, and I Timothy 2 were particularly troublesome to me and didn't seem to jibe with what Paul had said in **Galatians 3:28 — that in Christ, there is no Jew or Gentile, no slave or free, no male or female, for we are all one in Him.**

I wondered why Paul seemed so anti-woman in some of those passages. I became disenchanted, and no longer liked him. Did God love and respect women? Could women access God on their own, or did we need a husband? Suddenly Paul, whose writings on grace I had so cherished, didn't seem quite so friendly to me anymore. Instead, he frustrated me. He'd had this intense personal encounter with Jesus, wrote half the New Testament, and was an apostle for crying out loud, yet his epistles seemed to me to be at odds with the life of Jesus.

Jesus treated women with dignity, with respect, as though they were valuable. I couldn't understand why Paul deemed women less-than, in both marriage and church life, and for years I harbored a secret grudge against him. I didn't tell anyone. To say so seemed heretical, especially since his teaching on Grace had been so life-saving.

{Oddly enough, Peter gives similar instructions to Paul, but for some reason Peter never bothered me, possibly because he wrote less, or possibly because I had already connected so much with his unsteady walk of faith. Though in all fairness to Paul, Peter probably should have bothered me too.}

And this wasn't just about roles to me. **In my marriage, I've always experienced mutual love, respect, and equality, and in church I've always been able to find meaningful ministry to pursue.** So this wasn't about real-life grievances either. Rather, it was a more fundamental problem – it was about whether *God* thought I was important. After all, one of His chosen vessels, Paul, didn't seem to think so.

It was about needing assurance of God's love, and about whether my relationship with the Bible could withstand this storm. I was about to break fellowship with Paul over his view of women — basically, I was going to dump half the New Testament. I felt betrayed. The same Apostle whose words on Grace and salvation had been my rocks for years, was now turning on me. If he disrespected women, I didn't want to receive comfort and hope from his other words, either.

I knew I needed to make peace with this pillar of the early Church. I knew that if Paul disdained women – and by extension, that God disdained women – then I'd be out. I'd be done with this whole Jesus business, because I couldn't love and worship a God who made me a woman yet didn't love and value me on equal footing with men. If I'm going to follow God my whole life, I have to know I am worth something to Him. I needed this conflict to resolve, because I needed to love God.

I took my first tangible step towards reconciling with the apostle Paul on a Wednesday night in 2011. We visited lots of churches before moving overseas, and that night we were at Adrian Christian Church. Paul Burhart gave the devotional that night, and his words rocked my world. He was the first to give me some perspective on Ephesians 5, the classic text on authority in the marriage relationship.

Burhart described Ephesians 5 as a "race to the bottom." He said the well-known instruction to wives to submit means "to position under." But the instructions for the husband to "give up his life" like Jesus, mean "to surrender beside." This set-up sounded far more like equality to me, more like Eden, and much more similar to what I had experienced in my own marriage.
It's sort of like a Slinky on a stairstep, where the wife places herself under, and the husband follows her lead, by placing himself on the step below, where they are equal, and they continually repeat this process, mutually submitting to each other in love. It meant so much to me that I scribbled notes into my Bible, where they remain to this day.

Much later I would learn more specifically about Greco-Roman household codes and the subjugation women endured under that system. I learned that a woman was worth next to nothing in the 1st century A.D. I learned that a wife's submission to her husband as "lord" was already assumed at that time.

But Peter and Paul didn't just leave women to fend for themselves in this system. Instead, after they instructed women to do what they were already supposed to be doing in that culture anyway, they commanded the men to treat their wives, servants, and children with kindness, understanding, and love. It was nothing like the culture of the day, where men could treat their families however they wanted. **The new "Christian" culture Peter and Paul were introducing in their letters was totally revolutionary.**

{This is not to insinuate that all problematic passages (i.e. passages I don't personally like), are mere cultural conventions. But it does mean that Bible verses that seem anti-woman must be read in the context in which they were written – an extremely anti-woman society. Statements that seem harsh to my 21st century eyes might not be so harsh after all, especially when balanced with the rest of Scripture, including the many honored women in both the Old and New Testaments. And it also means that when I doubt God's love for me as a woman, maybe I should look just a little bit deeper than the surface.}

What Paul was doing in his letters was actually emancipating women and making men and women equal – a shocking thing to do in the environment of the early Church. But for too many years, I didn't know Paul was liberating men and women from rigid rules and roles, to be conformed to the image of the Son, in love, joy, and peace. When I understood some of the cultural background for the New Testament writers, I realized how countercultural Paul's teachings really were, and I began to love him again. **I could whole-heartedly embrace his teachings on grace again, knowing I was loved fully by the Father, that He created my inmost being lovingly and purposely, that my place in the Kingdom is secure, and the only mediator I need is Christ.**

In the end of my crisis of faith, I came to the conclusion that God considered me to have as much worth and value as any man. I came to believe that Christ's sacrifice redeems broken systems and broken relationships. And in the end, I came to believe that Paul believed that too. It was thus that I regained my trust in Paul, breaker of the bread of life and giver of the gospel of grace. And it was thus that I began to walk forward again as a child of God, as a Daughter of the King.

~~~~~~~~~~~~~~~~~~~~~~~~~~~~~~~~~~~~~~

Post Script: After I wrote this blog post, I read the book _Finally Feminist_. Author John G. Stackhouse, Jr. wrestles with both sides of the gender arguments — for we cannot pretend there are not seemingly opposing passages of Scripture regarding male-female relationships. Stackhouse deals with these issues through the lens of "the Kingdom now and not yet," and his treatment of the Bible helped me see the big picture of Sin and Redemption more clearly, and made me fall even more deeply in love with God. A very satisfying little book, and I can't recommend it highly enough.

WEAKER BUT EQUAL: HOW I FINALLY MADE PEACE WITH PETER

I've written before about how Paul's seemingly misogynistic passages were a real stumbling block to me at one time. In that post I mentioned that although Peter said some of the same things Paul said, he never bothered me quite the same way. Whether that's because I already liked Peter, who kept me laughing with all his mouth-moving-before-mind antics, or because he didn't write half the New Testament, so that his words didn't carry the same metaphorical weight, I'm not sure. I only know I should probably have dealt with his household codes before now. So I'm here today to offer you the latest in these apostolic adventures of mine.

First of all let me just say that I probably should have been asking more questions about Peter. For instance, where was his wife on all those missionary journeys?? I knew he had a wife, because I knew he had a mother-in-law, but I never asked the question – or, if I did, I assumed she stayed at home while he gallivanted all over Roman territory. (Perhaps I'd been too influenced by the more modern life of William Carey.)

Turns out, Peter's wife traveled with him. It's right there, plain as day, in I Corinthians 9:5 (which begs the question, how exactly did I miss this??). "Don't we have the right to bring a Christian wife with us as the other apostles and as the Lord's brothers do, and as Peter does?" So he *didn't* leave her at home. He valued her and brought her with him on his travels. (Many thanks to Michael Card for pointing this out in his commentary on Mark.)

Another thing Peter did? He took care of his mother-in-law, something I never questioned but that Card claimed wasn't Peter's cultural responsibility – it would have been his wife's brothers' responsibility. So it seems Peter valued his wife, and he valued his mother-in-law, and maybe just maybe he wasn't as anti-woman as I'd always thought, either.

In the past I'd kind of fixated on I Peter 3:1-6, with verses 5 and 6 giving me especial trouble as a trailing spouse:

In the same way, you wives must accept the authority of your husbands. Then, even if some refuse to obey the Good News, your godly lives will speak to them without any words. They will be won over by observing your pure and reverent lives. Don't be concerned about the outward beauty of fancy hairstyles, expensive jewelry, or beautiful clothes. You should clothe yourselves instead with the beauty that comes from within, the unfading beauty of a gentle and quiet spirit, which is so precious to God. This is how the holy women of old made themselves beautiful. They put their trust in God and accepted the authority of their husbands. For instance, Sarah obeyed her husband, Abraham, and called him her master. You are her daughters when you do what is right without fear of what your husbands might do.

Oh I knew that verse 7 existed, but maybe only in the New International or King James Versions, which are much more patronizing.

So anyway, prompted by Michael Card, I went and read all of I Peter 3, including verse 7 in the New Living Translation:

"In the same way, you husbands must give honor to your wives. Treat your wife with understanding as you live together. She may be weaker than you are, but she is your equal partner in God's gift of new life. Treat her as you should so your prayers will not be hindered."

And this Bible verse, this amazing, freeing, validating, liberating Bible verse, it was neither underlined nor starred in my Bible. WHY EVER NOT?!?! This is a Bible I've used for six years. Six years of reading the previous verses and feeling the weight of their burden, but never noticing verse 7 just below them?

These words are such a balm for my soul. Right there in verse 7 Peter calls me, as a wife, an equal partner. *An equal partner.* And this particular version tells husbands that they MUST give honor to their wives. Must?? That's a much more commanding tone than NIV or KJV.

So I did what I usually do when a verse strikes my fancy: I looked up the Greek words on Bible Hub.

- **Give** — to assign or apportion, to render; from the Greek aponemontes
- **Honor** – to accord or apportion honor, pay respect, perceived weight or value, from the Greek timen
- **Understanding** – knowledge, wisdom; from the Greek gnosin
- **Weaker** – weak, depleted, without sufficient strength (mostly physically); from the Greek asthenestero
- **Equal partner** – joint heir, participant, coinheritor; used of believers sharing inheritance with Christ; from the Greek synkleronomois
- **Hindered** – puts obstacles in the way of a moving object (this made me wonder, is the thing that the mistreatment of women hinders the movement of the Gospel?); to sharply impede or cut off what is desired or needed; from the Greek enkoptesthai

Basically, Peter is instructing husbands to assign appropriate honor and respect (there it is again, a woman's heart-need for respect) to their wives, because they are valuable and worthy, and to live with their wives in a wise and understanding way, because she is a joint heir, co-inheritor, and *equal partner* in Christ. And why should they do this? So the work of God won't be blocked or shortchanged in their lives.

Of course Eugene Peterson's *The Message* interpretation is even better:

"The same goes for you husbands: Be good husbands to your wives. Honor them, delight in them. As women they lack some of your advantages. But in the new life of God's grace, you're equals. Treat your wives, then, as equals so your prayers don't run aground."

But even if you stick with a strict translation and some Greek background, you will not get the same thing out of Peter that I have been getting for years (on the surface): a man at the top calling all the shots. Instead you will get: EQUAL PARTNER. A wife is her husband's *equal partner*.

It brings me to my knees in thanksgiving to have a Lord whose gospel of life reframes everything human beings tried to twist His perfect Edenic world into. So I'm now laying to rest my last reservation with Peter. Peter and I can now be completely at peace. And I can now rejoice that Peter — and God — calls me my husband's equal partner.

JESUS LOVES ME THIS I SOMETIMES KNOW

I used to think trusting God meant trusting Him for the circumstances of my life. I used to think it meant trusting God for my future. But this past year God has completely overhauled my understanding of Trust.

I'm married to a man who has **all the gifts**. Seriously. You name it, he's got it. And as he and his gifts have grown more public these past few years, I began to believe nobody valued my gifts or even noticed them. Nobody saw me, I told myself; they only saw *him*. I convinced myself the world didn't want anything I had to offer; they only wanted what *he* had to offer.

I felt myself disappearing, fading into nothingness. Very soon, I told myself, I would be invisible. *Am I important? Do I matter? Does anybody see me, truly see me?* In agony I flung these questions into the cosmos, only to have them answered time and again with a resounding NO. No, you're not seen; no, you don't matter; no, you're not important.

I was certain the problem was my marriage. If only I weren't married to such a massively talented man, I wouldn't feel this way. If only he would stop shining, I would feel better about myself. I accused him of *erasing me* and told him I wanted to die. **We kept repeating the same irrational conversations.**

Then one Sunday last fall I awoke with the sudden realization that **the bitterness I held toward my husband was actually directed at God.** None of this was my husband's fault — it was God's. He was the One who hadn't given me the desirable gifts. He was the One who was withholding from me. **This was no longer about my marriage: it was about my trust in God's goodness.**

Why does the Giver of gifts seem to pick favorites? Why are some people more highly favored? If God loves us all equally, why are His blessings so *unequal?* **Since (by my reckoning) God hadn't given me the good gifts, I concluded that He must not love me.**

110

That sounds ridiculous, I know. Learning that Jesus loves us is one of the first things we do in Sunday school. When we belt out *Jesus loves me, this I know, for the Bible tells me so*, we're supposed to believe it. Except here I was, and I didn't believe it.

I prayed a half-hearted prayer: *God, please, meet me at church today*. I'm not even sure I meant it. Then at church the speaker began talking about how God doesn't pick favorites. From my seat I remember hearing, "He doesn't like Ernie more than Ann." I looked up in astonishment and told God, *I think You just answered my prayer*.

God had spoken to my mind that morning, but my heart still had its doubts. My solution was to try grunting my way into belief. I thought if I just.tried.hard.enough, I could force myself to believe God's love for me. **But head knowledge has a hard time filtering down into heart knowledge, and I was groping in the dark.**

A few months later I found myself in a counseling office to debrief my first few years overseas. Conversation soon came to a standstill. I was stuck. The counselor wisely handed me some colored pencils and asked me to draw. I'm an abysmal artist, but I did as she asked: I drew a purple mountain's majesty, a part of Creation that draws me closer to God.

The counselor asked me what that mountain might say to me. The first words that came to me were "Just Sit." Then she asked what else that mountain might say to me, and the word "Believe" immediately flooded my soul.

"Believe what?" she asked.

Through tears, I croaked, "Believe that God loves me as much as He loves my husband."

And with that one word from God, months of striving to grasp His unconditional, all-surpassing, non-partisan Love evaporated. God used a poor colored-pencil sketch to short-circuit my rational brain and reach inside my heart. It was a breakthrough of belief that took me deeper into the love of God than I ever dreamed I'd go.

Shortly after my time with the counselor, I encountered I John 4:16 in the New International Version: **"And so we know and rely on the love God has for us."** I stopped cold. For me, knowing God's love came first, and relying on it came afterwards. How could this verse so perfectly sum up my experience of God's love when it had been written some 1,900 years earlier??

I loved this verse so much I looked it up in other versions. The English Standard Version reads, "And so we have come to know and to believe the love God has for us." When I looked it up in the Greek, I discovered that "know" implies a personal experience, and "believe" means to trust. **I John 4:16 is most definitely my story. First I had a personal experience of God's love, and now I find I can trust it.**

My Brute Force Method had failed. Trying to trust had failed. It was only when I let go and stopped striving that I could actually trust His love for me. So maybe trust is more of a release than a grip. Maybe it's more of an invitation than an instruction. **Maybe radical Trust in God isn't about my circumstances, but about His love.**

Psalm 13:5 declares, "I trust in Your unfailing love." Trust in His unfailing love is life to me now. I no longer believe the lies that tell me my husband is more valuable than I am. I know I'm loved, and I no longer need to slice through my husband's heart with my perfectly-practiced, precision-cut lies. **The most broken part of our marriage has been made whole. I never thought I'd be able to proclaim that.**

I am daily living Paul's prayer in Ephesians 3:17-19. I'm experiencing the love of Christ, and He is filling my life with His love. I'm trusting in Him, and He's making His home in my heart. **I feel my roots growing down deep into God's love, and I trust its width, length, height, and depth like never before.**

This is the cry of my heart for you today. I pray along with Paul, that "Christ will make His home in your hearts as you trust in Him. Your roots will grow down into God's love and keep you strong. And may you have the power to understand, as all God's people should, how wide, how long, how high, and how deep His love is. May you experience the love of Christ, though it is too great to understand fully. Then you will be made complete with all the fullness of life and power that comes from God."

*****

Further resources that helped me know and rely on the love God has for me:

The life and ministry of Rich Mullins, especially his song *"The Love of God"*

Anything by Brennan Manning, especially *"Reflections for Ragamuffins"*

10 WAYS TO CHOOSE LIFE IN THE MIDDLE OF AN EATING DISORDER

A couple years ago I taught a class to international teen girls which I entitled "Life After ED," with the term ED referring to eating disorders. I borrowed that title from a book I have not read because it so perfectly encapsulates what I want people to know: there *is* life after eating disorders. People need the hope of a life abundant when they're in the midst of a struggle with scarcity.

When we talk about eating disorders, we're talking about a range of struggles, including anorexia, bulimia, binge eating disorder, orthorexia (obsession with "right" eating), and eating disorders not otherwise specified (EDNOS). The research I've read indicates that 75% to 80% of women will deal with some sort of food or body image issue in their life, and many are easy to hide, so when I talk about eating disorders, I'm not just talking about extreme cases. Food and body image issues are struggles for all of us.

[Men deal with eating disorders too, but I don't know those stats, nor do I have significant knowledge of that subject.]

Most of the girls in that class were Third Culture Kids, and most of them didn't know my story. It feels like such a healed part of my life that I rarely think about it nowadays — and I often forget to tell it. So I started out by telling my personal story through the lens of a cross-cultural transition, because that was my experience. Then I touched on some theology regarding our bodies (including the concept of Imago Dei), and finished with a discussion of ways to seek healing and freedom in this area.

Today I'm only going to share some practical ways to choose life in the midst of a body image or food struggle. As I'm still in the early stages of truly understanding "the theology of the body" (yes that too is a borrowed book title), I'm going to skip that section of my class. And because I've published my eating disorder story before, I won't

114

rehash it here, even though the story I told these girls had some additional (and also very personal) details.

So without further ado, here's my list. And since this list is relatively short, feel free to ask for clarifications on any of the items, whether publicly or privately.

1. **Break the shackles of shame.** I want to take away the shame of struggling with these things. They're common to women. They're not terrible or shocking, whether it's to me or to God or to so many other women out there. So take a deep breath. These struggles with food and body hatred are just part of your life right now. The only way to move forward and get them out of your life is to acknowledge them. And remember, you are NOT alone.

2. **Get some help.** You really need some outside help to fight your food and body image battles. It's very hard to walk this path alone. So talk to someone – a parent, a counselor, a pastor, a teacher, another safe adult. But NOT a peer. Not a friend. It's not that you can't *confess* these things to your friends, but you can get into trouble partnering with a friend in fighting an eating disorder. It can become about competition. Or it can become about endorsement, where you and your friends all know you struggle, and you "accept" each other, but there is no accountability to grow or change. A counselor, on the other hand, will help you delve into the reasons why you stumbled into this eating disorder in the first place. A Christian counselor, in particular, will help you stand on the truth of God's word and seek Jesus for the healing of your mind and your body. But make sure your counselor feels safe to you. *If you're not comfortable with one, look for another.*

3. **Don't expect a quick fix.** There is no special prayer or special person's prayer that will magically and instantaneously cure your struggle. There is only consistently walking with Jesus toward healing and restoration and consistently realigning your mind with the truth of God's love. There is

only "a long obedience in the same direction" (to reference yet another book I haven't read).

4. **Don't be thrown off guard by relapses.** They are normal; I had three. Three separate times I stopped eating enough, lost too much weight, and stopped my normal female functioning too. It happened twice in high school and once after I had my second child. Remember, relapses are NOT the end of recovery or healing, and they don't mean that no healing or recovery has occurred. They are just a temporary setback. So take a deep breath and start again to walk this road of healing.

5. **Don't get your ideas of what your body is supposed to look like from magazines or images on the internet.** This is simple to understand but *difficult* to live. I know how tempting it is to look at those pictures and compare yourself to them. I know how tempting it is to compare yourself to your own personal idea of a perfect body. But those images, whether on a screen or on a glossy magazine page, or inside your own head, don't tell the truth. They aren't real. Don't let them lie to you about what is beautiful or valuable or what you must look like. Reject those ideas, they're not from God. Put down the magazines or turn off your phone or your computer if you have to.

6. **Know where your value and worth come from.** When God formed us from the dust, He stamped us with His image, something He didn't do for any other creature. This is the idea of *imago dei*: the belief that all human beings, regardless of status or creed or "usefulness" or even likability, are valuable, because the God who created them is the one who gives them their value. *Imago dei* is what needs to be restored when we struggle with disordered eating, body image distortion, body shame, body hatred, or the effects of sexual abuse. So remember how much you are worth — body, soul, and all.

7. **Look in the mirror and declare God's Word over yourself.** This can be really hard and uncomfortable at first. Get into your underclothes and stand in front of that mirror and speak *out loud* statements like, "I am fearfully and wonderfully made," or "I am created in the image of God, and God himself says that's very good," or "I am a child of God," or "I am in Christ Jesus, and there is no condemnation for me, not even from myself," or "The Spirit is setting me free from these things." It's hard at this stage to accept your physical body as something *good*, but try practicing these things and see if they help.

8. **Work on portion control, but avoid calorie counting.** Portion control can be hard. Whether you're accustomed to restricting OR overeating, it's difficult to learn to listen to your body's signs of hunger and fullness and to eat a normal, regular amount of food that's not too big and not too small. Look up recommended portion sizes if you want, but don't pay too much attention to calorie counts. Calorie counting is both legalistic and addictive and tends to be used in fear, not freedom. So don't get hung up on calories.

9. **Hold onto hope for healing, restoration, and life abundant.** I stand before you today free of obsessive thoughts of body hatred. I may have occasional thoughts of dissatisfaction, but I am free of obsession and the accompanying depression that my body is not good enough (and that therefore *I* am not good enough). So I want you to have HOPE: hope for freedom and wholeness and a full life after dealing with eating disorders.

10. **Remember that God is not giving up on you.** God longs to live in you, in body, soul, and spirit. He will not give up on you, no matter how many times you binge, purge, or starve. He loves you the SAME. Always the same, eternal, everlasting, pure, perfect love. Of course we will make mistakes and let our beliefs and thoughts get all messed up. Of course we will make mistakes and make poor

choices: *that's why Jesus came.* God knew we would need Him, and He never gives up on us.

ON NOT BEING THE CASSEROLE LADY

Many a Casserole Lady has cared for me. The Casserole Lady brings food to the hurting, nourishment to the weary, comfort to the downcast. She's first on your doorstep with home-baked bread and brownies, with meatloaf and soup, and of course, with casseroles galore. She ensures you don't need to plan and prepare meals when you're grieving a loss, are freshly postpartum, or find yourself in any other time of need.

I love the Casserole Ladies, but I am not one of them.

Sometimes I think about people with the gift of hospitality and get this gnawing, guilty feeling. Why can't I be more like them? I wish I could, for hospitality seems like the Real Spiritual Gift. Delivering meals to doorsteps, inviting large groups into your home for meals, hosting people long-term as part of your family — this all sounds *so very first century Christian*. I sigh and start to think I must not measure up.

But I think my accounting system is off when I calculate this way. Maybe I shouldn't be tallying things up like this. It shouldn't be about *me, me, me*. It shouldn't be about how valuable or useful *my* gifts are. We shouldn't have a "usefulness hierarchy" — that's a joy-stealer if ever I heard one. Instead, I've come to believe that it's about the *love behind* my actions. **It's about my offering of love to the Lord's Beloved, for I speak a language of love to the Church that is no less than those gifted in hospitality.**

This idea of speaking a language of love originated in Gary Chapman's book "The Five Love Languages," where he specifies these 5 love languages:

Words of Affirmation
Physical Touch
Acts of Service
Gifts

119

I've mostly heard the idea of Love Languages applied to individual relationships, and to marriage in particular. It generally seems to be discussed in the context of getting your own needs met, explaining why you're disappointed when they aren't, and of course making sure you meet your spouse's needs in return. [Note: I'm *not* saying that's how it's discussed in the book. I'm just saying that's how I've usually heard it discussed amongst The People.]

That approach just doesn't satisfy me anymore. I want to reframe the gifts discussion, and I want to reframe the love language discussion. I want to stop talking about the gifts we receive *from* God and start talking about the love we offer back *to* Him. I want to move beyond just determining how I prefer to *receive* love, and start embracing the way I most wholeheartedly *give* love.
Some people, like the Casserole Ladies, love through their Acts of Service. (And we're all grateful for them!)

Some people love through monetary Gifts. (And building funds and charities everywhere are grateful for them, not to mention those of us in support-based ministry who rely on Gifts for our daily bread.)

Some people love through Physical Touch. (And we're all grateful for the huggers and the greeters and, let's not forget, the tireless nursery workers and stay-at-home moms.)

Some people love through Quality Time. (And we're all grateful for the preachers, teachers, and small group leaders who painstakingly prepare lessons week after week, and for those who sit with people, whether sick or well, whether discouraged or not, giving their time to them.)

Obviously this is not an exhaustive treatise on all the ways members of the Body might speak these five different love languages! I just want to ask this question today: **How do you speak love, out of an overflow of your own heart, to the Church?** Not what you *think* you should be doing to serve. Not what you see someone else doing. Not what you've always done. **But, how do you speak love in such a way that brings you joy?**

For me, the way I most wholeheartedly give love to the Body of Christ is through Words of Affirmation. I use words with the hope of blessing people, not for my sake, but for theirs. I offer words, and not just in blog posts — though they're here too. I also pour all my love into emails and private messages, just because I want to, and because it brings me joy. It is through words that I give gladly and love fully.

I take my counsel from Peter, who says "Do you have the gift of speaking? Then speak as though God himself were speaking through you," and from Paul, who says, "If your gift is to encourage others, be encouraging." I hear their commission to speak and encourage not through the lens of gift or skill or talent, but through the lens of love.

I want the discussion of love languages to be about what we give, *for the pure joy of it*, and not what we need from others. I want to approach service from the vantage point of love, and not of giftings. Not from a focus on *me* and what God has given *me*, but from a focus on offering my love to others. Not in order to pigeonhole myself into speaking only one "language," but to embrace the way I show love and to give my whole soul to it.

I want our love languages to be an outpouring of love, a breaking open of our alabaster boxes.

What is your offering of love to the Church? What Language do you speak to her?

Check out Julie Meyer's song *Alabaster Box,* in which she talks about pouring out all her love for Jesus.

~~~~~~~~~~~~~~~~~~~~~~~~~~~~~~~~~

And we cannot end without a quote from Henri Nouwen who, in his book _The Return of the Prodigal Son_, expresses my feelings and experiences so well:

"When I first saw Rembrandt's painting, I was not as familiar with the home of God within me as I am now. Nevertheless, my intense response to the father's embrace of his son told me that I was desperately searching for that inner place where I too could be held as safely as the young man in the painting. . . .

I have a new vocation now. It is the vocation to speak and write from that place back into the many places of my own and other people's restless lives. I have to kneel before the Father, put my ear against his chest and listen, without interruption, to the heartbeat of God. Then, and only then, can I say carefully and very gently what I hear.

I know now that I have to speak from eternity into time, from the lasting joy into the passing realities of our short existence in this world, from the house of love into the houses of fear, from God's abode into the dwellings of human beings. I am well aware of the enormity of this vocation. Still, I am confident that it is the only way for me."

THAT TIME PAUL TALKED ABOUT BREASTFEEDING

My husband and I worked in local church ministry for over ten years before moving abroad to serve for the last five and a half. There's something I want you to know about this life: you're going to need a lot of fortitude for the journey. Working with people, in any time and any place, is hard. It doesn't matter if it's in your home country or a host country. Working with people is heart-wrenching and soul-filling, and you need endurance.

This is something else I want you to know: **in the years ahead, never hesitate to serve out of your feminine strength.** A lot of teaching models are filled with masculine metaphors. There's battle this, and army that. There's fighting here and soldiering on there. The Bible itself is filled with battle-speak. We are to put on the full armor of God so that we can take our stand against the devil's schemes. But the same Paul who told us in Ephesians 6 that our battle is not against flesh and blood and that we were to arm ourselves and stay alert and be persistent and stand firm, that very same **Paul was not ashamed in his first letter to the Thessalonians to compare himself to a woman.**

In I Thessalonians 2:7, Paul, Silas and Timothy jointly describe their conduct among the believers there: **"We were gentle among you, like a nursing mother taking care of her own children" (ESV).** I was in a training session this summer when I first truly took hold of this verse. We had studied the great faith and love of the Thessalonian church in chapter 1, and now we were in chapter 2 studying the attributes of the men who'd told them the Good News. When we got to the verse about these three men acting like a mother, some of the men seemed to want to brush it off and focus instead on verse 11, where the letter writers compare themselves to good fathers.

But I couldn't brush Paul's words off. I remembered how physically demanding it was to be a nursing mother. I had to speak out: _'We have this idea of a mother with her nursing baby that's all sweetness and light. But it's not. It's really hard work. You have to feed yourself well, so you can feed_ *your baby. You have to get up at all hours of the night to care for a crying child, and you have to try not to be cranky about all that lost sleep."*

As I spoke, women all around me nodded their heads in agreement, and several told me afterward how glad they were that I had said that. They had lived it, too, and they knew the challenges of mothering. You need a lot of stamina. You don't sleep through the night for months on end. Sometimes you get painful mastitis or yeast infections. You have to keep up your water and calorie intake. To your embarrassment, you leak milk everywhere. Or you have to work hard to make *enough* milk. Sometimes you can't figure out for the life of you how to make this child stop crying, but somehow you have to stay calm while you do it. On top of that, you're basically tethered to your child because you don't know when they'll need to eat again. **You sacrifice many things for this child, this child whom you love so tenderly and so fiercely.**

Somehow this was something the apostle Paul understood. When we serve people, we have to make sure we're getting our spiritual nourishment first, before we can pass anything of value on to them. Living and working among the continual, desperate needs of other people can physically and emotionally deplete us. And sometimes other people's needs interrupt our planned and preferred schedules. Paul knew all this. He lived all this. At the same time, Paul felt incredible affection for the Thessalonians. Paul, Silas, and Timothy loved them so much that they shared not only the good news with them, but their own lives as well (verse 8). And they'd spent plenty of time praising them in the chapter before.

Over the past few months I have been unable to let verse 7 go. I've learned that in the Greek, the noun was unmistakably feminine. It was *trophos*: a care-giver, a person sustaining someone else by nourishing and offering the tender care of a nurse. I've learned that it had the connotation of mother's care, of holding a child close, wrapped in her arms. There is familiarity here. Affection. Tenderness. The verb was *thalpo*: to cherish, nourish, foster, comfort, nurture, or keep warm. There is action here, decision, deliberate investment. And the phrase "her own children" (*heautou teknon*) indicates belonging. An inclusion. A turning towards.

All of these feminine-sounding words can illuminate our own roles, wherever God has placed us. They are not weakness. They are not unnecessary or irrelevant or dispensable. They are strength and they are resiliency and they are *essential*. Whether or not you've ever been a nursing mother, you have a yearning for relationship that can solidify your ministry, not undermine it. Whether or not you've ever been a nursing mother, you have an instinct to care for people sacrificially. Whether or not you've ever been a nursing mother, you have the capacity to lead with endurance.

Paul wasn't ashamed of these qualities, and neither should we be. It is good and healthy to identify as a woman and serve out of our God-given identity. Of course, men can be nurturers too – just see verse 11. And women can be warriors – just see Deborah. But when I read these verses, I feel so much validation. Validation of my work and validation of my worth. All those years living and ministering as a woman, they weren't wasted. And as someone who has had a **<u>fraught relationship</u>** with the Apostle Paul over the years, these verses are yet one more reason I can love both him and his letters, **for he wasn't afraid to lean into the feminine for the sake of the people he was serving**. It is something we needn't be afraid of either.

ABOUT THE AUTHOR

Elizabeth is the editor-in-chief for the missions website, A Life Overseas (alifeoverseas.com). She also writes regularly at trotters41.com and Velvet Ashes (velvetashes.com).

After a military childhood, a teenaged Elizabeth crash landed onto American civilian life. When she married her high school sweetheart, her life plan was to be a chemical engineer while he practiced law. Instead, they both fell headlong into youth ministry and spent the next ten years serving the local church. When her husband later decided he wanted to move overseas, Elizabeth didn't want to join him. Now, after six years of life in Cambodia, she can't imagine doing anything else. Elizabeth loves math, science, and all things Jane Austen. Days find her homeschooling her four children, while nights find her eating hummus by the spoonful.

Made in the USA
Monee, IL
25 February 2023

28703912R00080